T0337645

ANIMAL AMIGURUMI ADVENTURES

VOLUME II

15 (More!) Crochet Patterns to Create Adorable Amigurumi Critters

BY LAUREN ESPY

DEDICATION

In memory of my sweet mom, Shannon. You always encouraged me to go for my dreams and were my biggest cheerleader through it all.

TABLE OF CONTENTS

INTRODUCTION

Hi friends!
I'm so thrilled to have you back for another adventure! I hope the monkeys didn't give you too much trouble on our last trip!

Before we begin I just wanted to take a moment to introduce myself in case you're new around here. My name is Lauren and I'm the crochet designer behind A Menagerie of Stitches. I'm a full-time crochet designer and author who is obsessed with all things crochet, especially amigurumi.

My love for amigurumi has always stemmed from being able to create fun toys for all ages to enjoy. Growing up I was always doing arts and crafts with my mom and grandma so it's always been something I have truly enjoyed. When I taught myself how to crochet back in 2009, I had no idea that amigurumi would, in fact, be the thing that would change my life. Being able to create crochet patterns for food, plants, animals, you name it, has been such a huge part of my life that I absolutely love sharing with the world.

For this book, I wanted to do something I hadn't done much of before and that was to create adorable animals! Animals are amazing creatures and I loved getting to learn more about them as I crocheted each one. Just like in *Animal Amigurumi Adventures Volume 1*, we'll explore three different locations and see five animals in each location that call that area home.

Our journey starts with a trip to the safari to feed the giraffes and watch the hippos play. Bundle up! Our quest continues all the way to the arctic where we make friends with the penguins and an adorable walrus. Before we head home, we stop by the pet shop to see all the furry friends up for adoption.

As you navigate through this book, I hope you find your favorite animal or discover a few new ones to love. Customize them by choosing your favorite yarn colors or adding little embellishments. The possibilities are endless!

I'm ready for this next adventure and can't wait to take you all along with me. Pack your yarn and crochet hooks and let's go meet some seriously cute animals!

Happy crocheting!

Lauren

TOOLS & MATERIALS

YARN

There are many different types of yarns to choose from, but my favorite for amigurumi is a worsted weight acrylic. Worsted weight is referred to as a level 4, or medium weight yarn. I like using acrylic because it comes in lots of different colors, is affordable, and works great for making amigurumi. Choose your favorite brands and colors for the animals in this book!

For a list of the specific brands and exact colors I used throughout this book, please visit my website, www.amenagerieofstitchesblog.com

CROCHET HOOK

Crochet hooks come in a variety of sizes and can be made from aluminum, plastic, or wood. I typically grab an aluminum hook with an ergonomic handle, as this feels best in my hand while crocheting. Make sure to pick a hook that works and feels comfortable in your hand.

To keep it simple, all the patterns in this book will use a F/3.75mm crochet hook. Of course, you may choose to use a larger or smaller hook, if you prefer. Just be aware that your animals could turn out smaller or larger depending on the hook size you use.

SAFETY EYES

Safety eyes come in a wide variety of sizes and colors. They have a plastic or metal washer that attaches to the back of the eye once inserted into the crocheted piece. Make sure you have positioned the eyes exactly where you would like before attaching the backs, as they are impossible to remove once attached. Buttons, felt, or embroidered eyes are a great alternative to safety eyes.

For the patterns in this book, we will be using solid black eyes in the following sizes: 8mm, 10mm, 10.5mm, and 12mm. If you plan on giving the items you make to small children, I always recommend replacing the safety eyes with felt or embroidering them on with yarn or embroidery floss.

FIBERFILL STUFFING

Polyester fiberfill is great for stuffing amigurumi. Make sure to add enough so that the piece will hold its shape, but be sure to not overstuff. Adding too much will cause the stitches to stretch and the fiberfill to show through. Use a chopstick or the end of a crochet hook to help get fiberfill into smaller parts that your fingers can't reach.

YARN NEEDLE

An essential part of amigurumi! Also called a darning or tapestry needle, yarn needles are ideal for sewing pieces together or weaving in ends. They have a blunt tip and a much larger eye, making it super easy to thread yarn onto it.

STITCH MARKERS

Stitch markers are a must when making amigurumi! Because we will be crocheting in the round, we'll need to use one of these to mark the end of the previous round. Alternatively, you can use a contrasting piece of yarn or a safety pin instead.

EMBROIDERY NEEDLE AND FLOSS

These are used for adding the finer details to amigurumi, like mouths and noses. I like to use embroidery floss when adding these details because it comes in so many different colors and is a lot thinner than yarn. For the projects in this book, we'll be using black, white, and brown embroidery floss.

SCISSORS

A sharp pair of scissors will come in handy for cutting out felt shapes or trimming yarn and embroidery floss.

STRAIGHT PINS

Before assembling the pieces of your animal, use straight pins to position the items. This will help you make sure your items are right where you want them before you commit to sewing them on.

FELT

I love using felt to add small details and texture to an animal. Things like noses and eyes can be easily made using different colored felt. Use a hot glue gun or embroidery floss to attach the felt to the crocheted pieces. For these projects, we'll be using black, white, brown, and tan felt.

PIPE CLEANERS

Pipe cleaners (also known as chenille stems) are perfect for adding stability and bend to an item. We will be using pipe cleaners in the tail and feet for the Chameleon pattern found in the Pets chapter (page 136).

HOT GLUE GUN

I love using a hot glue gun to attach felt or crocheted details to a piece. The outcome is always much cleaner and gives the animal a polished look. The trick is to go slow and only add a little bit of glue at a time. Gluing these kinds of details in place is much faster than sewing. If you prefer to not use hot glue, sewing with embroidery floss and a needle is a great alternative.

PET SLICKER BRUSH

One of my favorite tools to use! Using a pet slicker brush helps fluff up the yarn and give the piece a different texture. Use this brush on the tail of the Lion (page 56).

ABBREVIATIONS

All patterns in this book are written using U.S. crochet terminology.

BLO - Back Loops Only
Bo - Bobble
Ch - Chain
Dc - Double Crochet
Dc Inc - Double Crochet Increase
Dec - Decrease
FLO - Front Loops Only
Hdc - Half Double Crochet
Hdc Inc - Half Double Crochet Increase
Inc - Increase
Inv Dec - Invisible Decrease
Mini Bo - Mini Bobble
Mr - Magic Ring
R - Round or Row
Sc - Single Crochet
Sl St - Slip Stitch
St/s - Stitch/es
Tr - Treble Crochet
Tr Inc - Treble Crochet Increase
Yo - Yarn Over

* - Repeat the steps between asterisks as many times as stated.
( ) - The number inside the parentheses will indicate how many stitches you will have at the end of the round or row.

STITCHES & TECHNIQUES

For extra help, video tutorials on how to do these stitches can be found on my blog, www.amenagerieofstitchesblog.com, and on my YouTube channel, A Menagerie of Stitches.

GAUGE

While gauge is an important step in crocheting, for amigurumi it isn't too important. Everyone holds the yarn differently, so your tension may be different than mine. Make sure your tension is even throughout and that your stitches aren't too loose, allowing the fiberfill to show through. Keep in mind that using a smaller or larger hook size and different yarn will change the size of your toys. Measurements for each project are given and are a rough estimate of what the finished sizes will be.

YARN OVER (YO)

To yarn over, simply take your hook and grab hold of the yarn. The yarn will go from the back to the front of the hook. (photo 1) The yarn will be going over your hook, and then you can proceed to pull it through the loop or stitch.

MAGIC RING (MR)

To make a magic ring:

1. Make a loop and place the working yarn on top of the loose tail. (photo 1)
2. Insert hook into loop, grabbing the working yarn with the hook. Pull through the loop. (photos 2+3)
3. Yarn over and pull hook through loop. This is considered a "Ch 1." (photos 4+5)
   This next step is where you will start making single crochets into the magic ring.
4. Insert the hook back into the loop, making sure to go underneath both loops. (photo 6)
5. Yarn over and pull hook through loop. 2 loops will be on the hook. (photos 7+8)

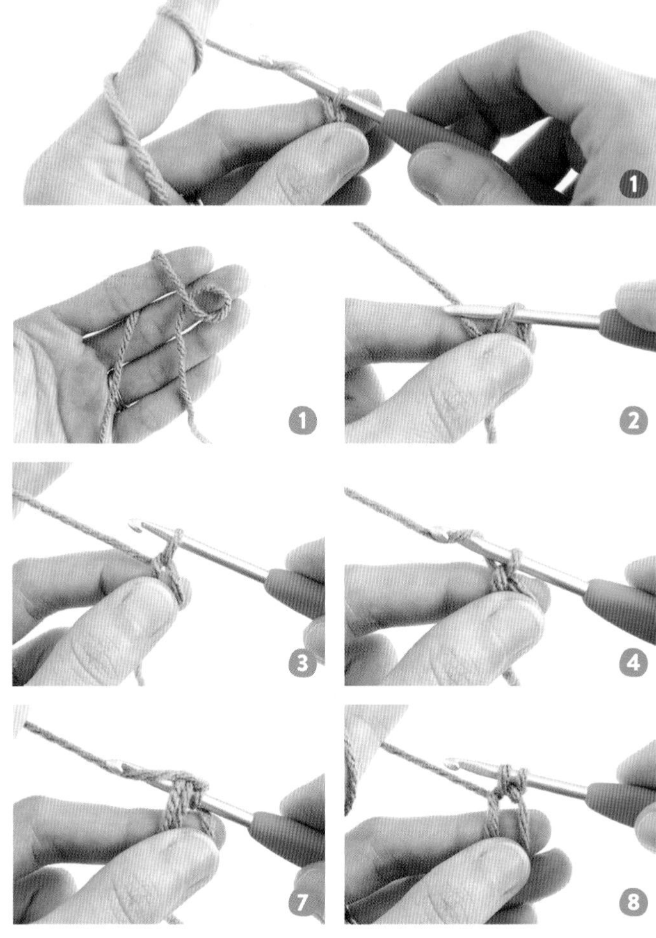

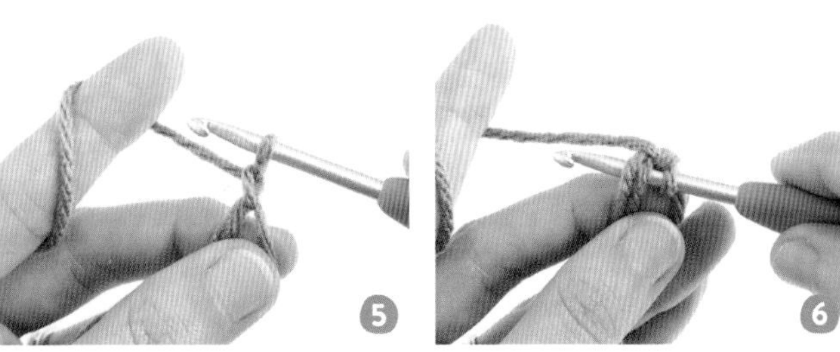

6. Yarn over and pull through both loops. 1 loop will remain on the hook. This completes your first single crochet. (photo 9)
7. Repeat steps 4-6 as many times as pattern states. Most patterns state to do six single crochets in a magic ring. (photo 10)
8. Finally, grab the loose tail and pull to close the loop. You now have a completed magic ring. (photo 11)

To begin the next round, place the next stitch into the first single crochet made in step 6. (photo 12)

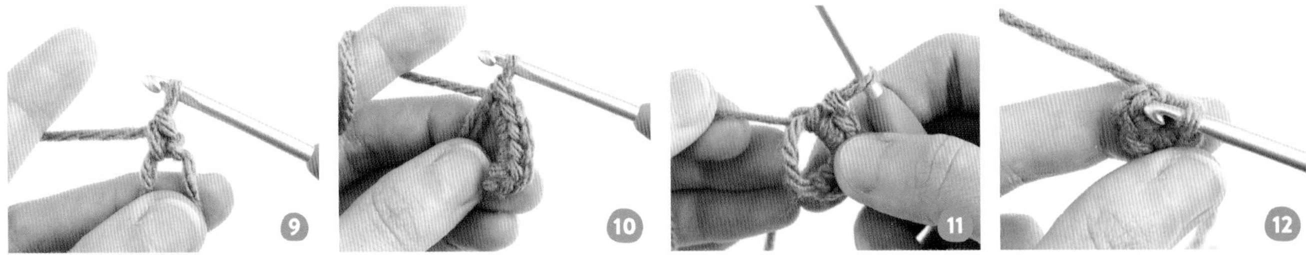

SINGLE CROCHET (SC)

1. Insert hook into stitch and yarn over. (photos 1+2)
2. Pull hook through stitch. There will be 2 loops on your hook. (photo 3)
3. Yarn over again and pull through both loops. 1 loop will remain on hook. (photos 4+5)

INCREASE (INC)

An increase is used to expand your piece and make it bigger. To increase, simply place 2 single crochets into 1 stitch. If you look at the photo, you'll see 2 "Vs" in one stitch. (photo 1) This is an increase.

HALF DOUBLE CROCHET (HDC)

1. Yarn over and insert hook into stitch. (photos 1+2)
2. Yarn over and pull hook through stitch. 3 loops will remain on the hook. (photos 3+4)
3. Yarn over and pull through all 3 loops. 1 loop will remain on the hook. (photos 5+6)

DOUBLE CROCHET (DC)

1. Yarn over and insert hook into stitch. (photos 1+2)
2. Yarn over and pull hook through stitch. 3 loops will remain on the hook. (photos 3+4)
3. Yarn over and pull through 2 loops only. 2 loops will remain on the hook. (photos 5+6)
4. Yarn over for a final time and pull hook through remaining 2 loops. 1 loop will remain on the hook. (photos 7+8)

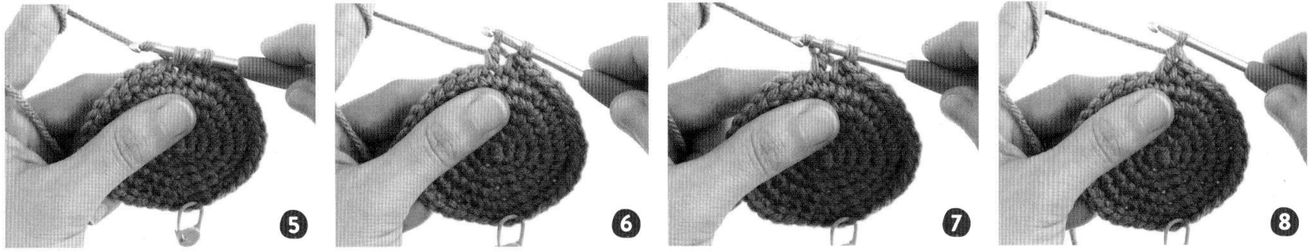

TREBLE CROCHET (TR)

1. Yarn over 2 times so that 3 loops are on the hook. (photo 1)
2. Insert hook into stitch and yarn over. (photo 2)
3. Pull hook through stitch. There will be 4 loops on your hook. (photo 3)
4. Yarn over and pull through 2 loops. 3 loops will remain on the hook. (photos 4+5)
5. Yarn over again and pull through another 2 loops. 2 loops will remain on the hook. (photos 6+7)
6. Yarn over for a final time and pull through the remaining 2 loops. 1 loop will remain on the hook. (photo 8)

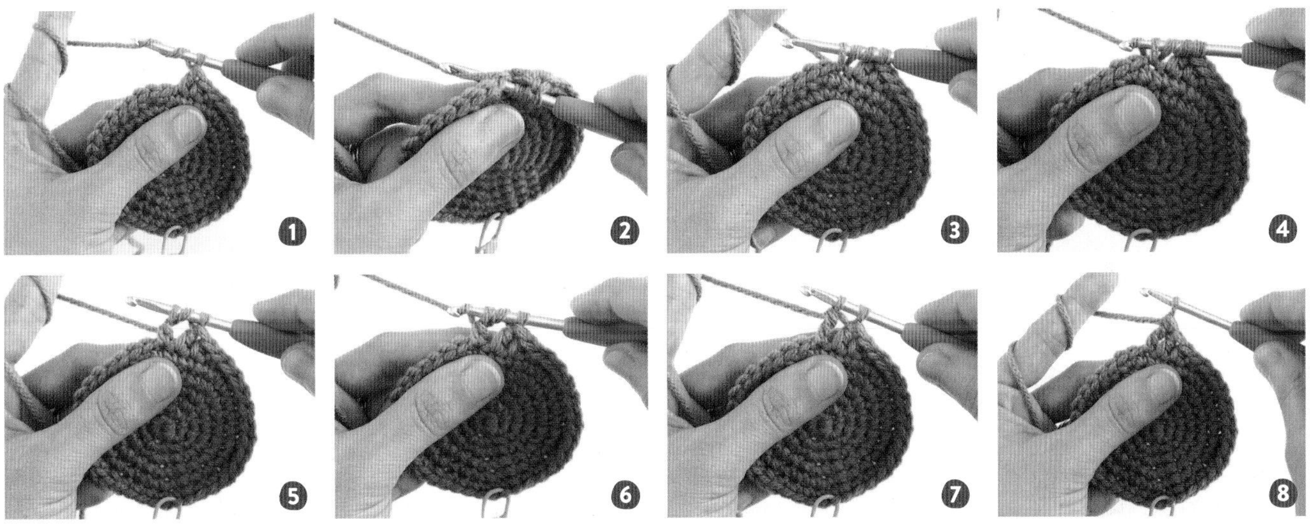

HALF DOUBLE CROCHET, DOUBLE CROCHET, TREBLE CROCHET INCREASE (HDC INC, DC INC, TR INC)

These are just like the regular single crochet increase. Simply place 2 half double crochet stitches, 2 double crochet stitches, or 2 treble crochet stitches into one stitch to create the increase.

INVISIBLE DECREASE (INV DEC)

This is my favorite way to decrease amigurumi. A normal decrease tends to add a little bulk to the finished piece, whereas an invisible decrease is nearly impossible to spot.

To invisible decrease:

1. Insert the hook into the FRONT loops only of the next 2 stitches. There will be 3 loops on your hook. (photo 1)
2. Yarn over and pull hook through the 2 front loops. 2 loops will remain on the hook. (photos 2+3)
3. Yarn over again and pull through the 2 remaining loops. 1 loop will remain on the hook. (photo 4)

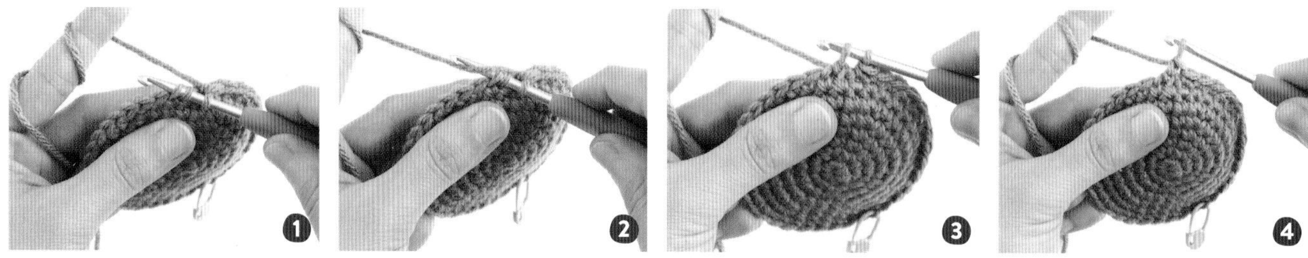

REGULAR DECREASE (DEC)

A couple patterns use this technique for decreasing, which is mainly used when working flat pieces and not in the round.

To make a regular decrease:

1. Insert the hook into the next stitch. Yarn over and pull hook through. There will be 2 loops on the hook. (photos 1+2)
2. Insert the hook into the next stitch. Yarn over and pull hook through. There will be 3 loops on the hook. (photos 3-5)
3. Yarn over for the last time and pull through all 3 loops. 1 loop will remain on the hook. (photos 6+7)

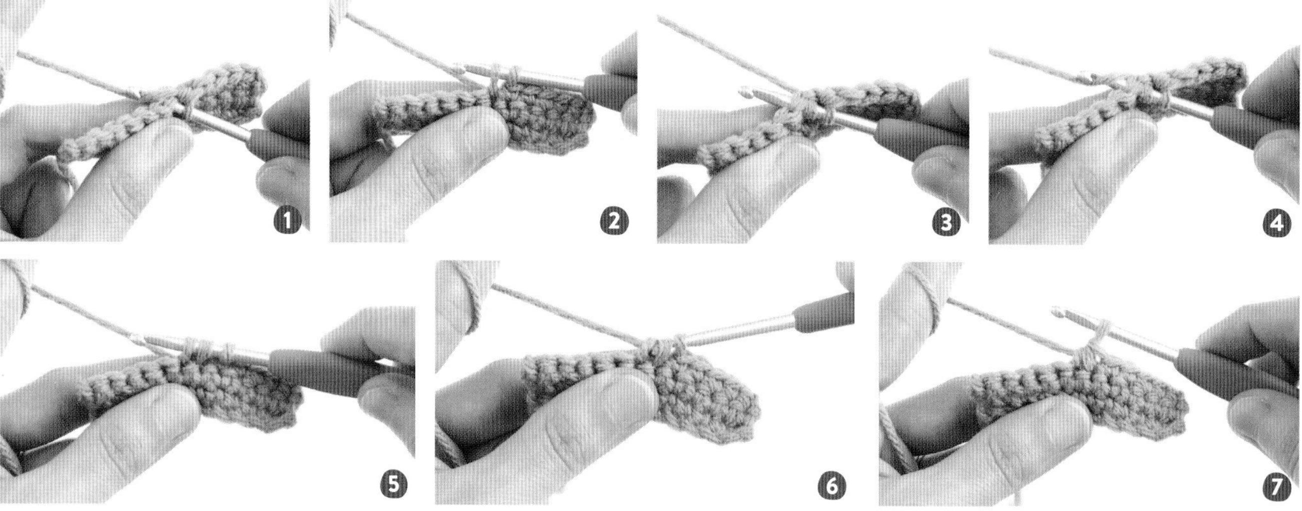

SLIP KNOT

1. Make a loop and place the loose tail on top of the working yarn. (photo 1)
2. Insert hook into loop and grab the loose tail. (photos 2+3)
3. Pull the loose tail through the loop. (photo 4)
4. Holding both tails, pull to tighten the slip knot onto the hook. (photo 5)

CHAIN (CH)

1. After you have made a slip knot, simply take the working yarn and yarn over. (photo 1)
2. Pull hook through the slip knot. This is your first chain stitch. Repeat as many times as the pattern states. (photos 2+3)

SLIP STITCH (SL ST)

1. Insert hook into stitch or chain and yarn over. (photos 1-3)
2. Pull hook through the stitch or chain. There will be 2 loops on your hook. (photo 4)
3. Pull hook through the first loop. 1 loop will remain on hook. (photos 5+6)

FRONT OR BACK LOOPS ONLY (FLO OR BLO)

Some of the patterns in this book use this technique. When holding your work, you'll see from the top that the stitches look like a sideways "V". The side closest to you is the front loop (photo 1), and the one behind is the back loop. (photo 2) When the pattern states to crochet "In FLO", work the stitches in the front loops only. (photo 3) After crocheting a few stitches, you'll notice the back loops are visible since we aren't working in them. (photo 4) When the pattern states to crochet "In BLO", insert hook into the center of the V, going under the back loop. (photo 5) Again, after a few stitches made in the back loops, you'll notice the front loops are visible. (photo 6)

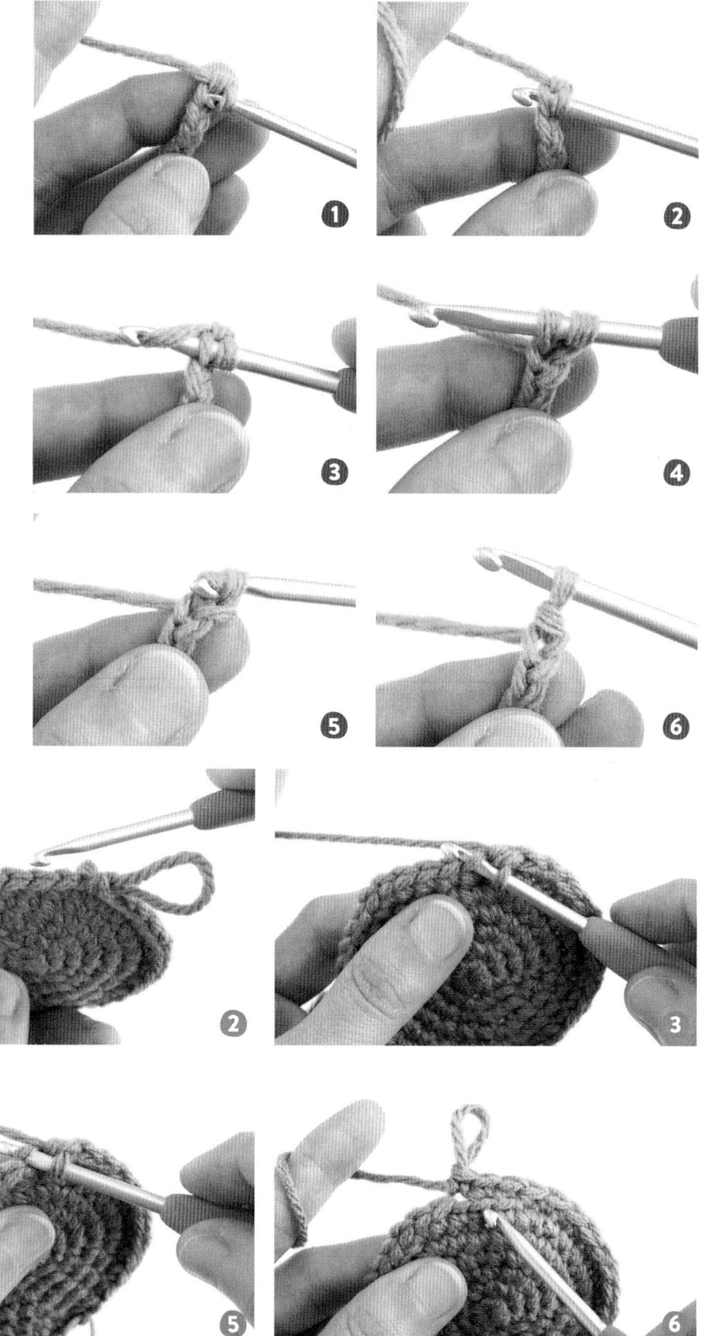

BOBBLE STITCH (BO)

1. Yarn over and insert hook into stitch. (photos 1+2)
2. Yarn over and pull hook through the same stitch. There will be 3 loops on your hook. (photo 3)
3. Yarn over and pull through the first 2 loops. 2 loops will remain on your hook. (photos 4+5)
4. Repeat steps 1-3 a total of 4 more times until there are 6 loops on your hook. (photo 6)
5. Yarn over and pull through all loops on hook. 1 loop will remain on your hook. (photos 7+8)

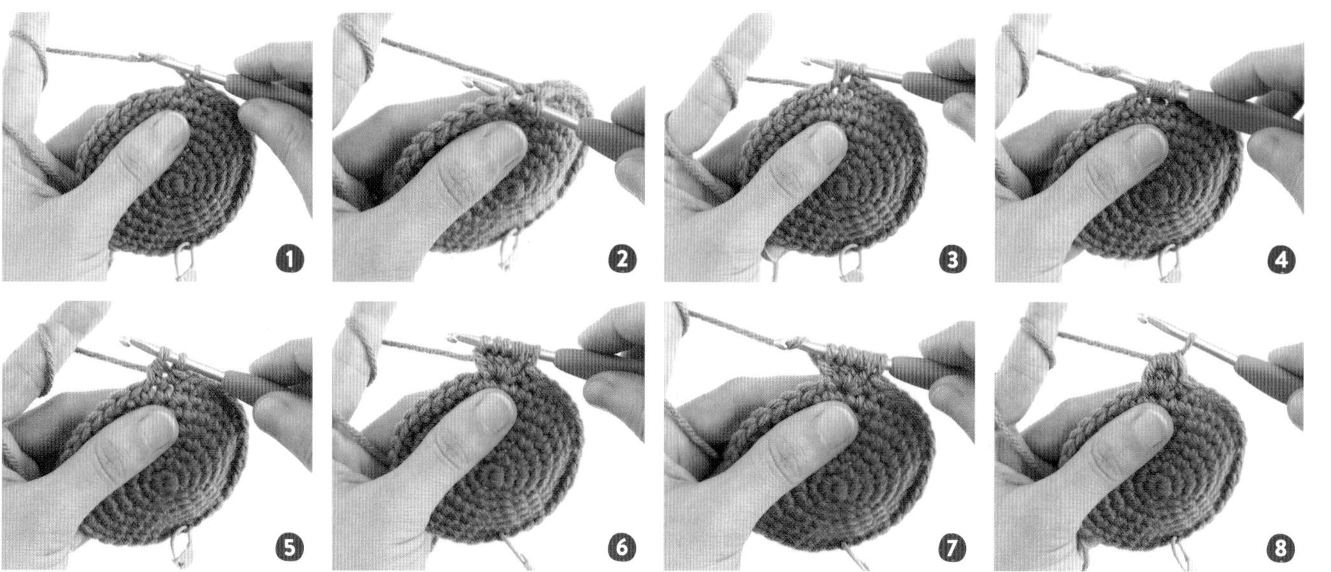

MINI BOBBLE (MINI BO)

1. Yarn over and insert hook into stitch. (photos 1+2)
2. Yarn over and pull hook through the same stitch. There will be 3 loops on your hook. (photo 3)
3. Yarn over and pull through the first 2 loops. 2 loops will remain on your hook. (photos 4+5)
4. Repeat steps 1 and 2 once more until there are 3 loops on your hook. (photo 6)
5. Yarn over and pull through all loops on hook. 1 loop will remain on your hook. (photos 7+8)

CLEAN COLOR CHANGE

A clean color change is used when you don't want the color change to be as noticeable. While the color change is still visible, it's a lot less drastic.

1. When working the last stitch of the old color, single crochet until there are just 2 loops left on the hook. (photo 1)
2. Use the new color to yarn over and complete the stitch. (photos 2+3)
3. Slip stitch into the next stitch with the new color. (photos 4-6)
4. Continue to crochet as normal with the new color. (photo 7)

Trim the tail of the old color. Tie the tails from both colors together to secure the color change. I used this method for the Zebra (page 66) and Penguin (page 90).

REGULAR COLOR CHANGE

A regular color change is great if you want the color change to be more visible. By doing this method, the stitch in the new color is more noticeable than if you were to use the "Clean Color Change" method.

Use this method on the bodies of the Chameleon (page 136) and Guinea Pig (page 164).

1. When working the last stitch of the old color, single crochet until there are just 2 loops left on the hook. (photo 1)

2. Use the new color to yarn over and complete the stitch. (photos 2+3)
3. Single crochet into the next stitch and continue crocheting as normal with the new color. (photos 4+5)

Trim the tail of the old color. Tie the tails from both colors together to secure the color change.

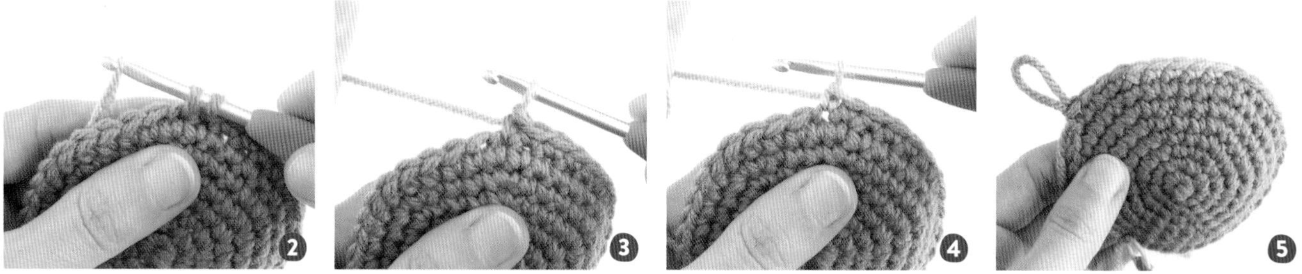

RIGHT SIDE/WRONG SIDE OF WORK

When working your pieces, you'll notice that one side will always be facing you. This side is considered the "right" side of the work. The side facing away from you is the "wrong" side, or the back side of the work. One way to decipher which side is which is to simply look at the side facing you and look for the "V". (photo 1) If you turn your work over to the back side, you'll notice that there is a horizontal bar in between each row of "V's". (photo 2) Sometimes the work tends to curl in the opposite direction, which causes the "wrong" side of the work to end up on the outside of the finished piece. If it does curl, just make sure to correct it so the "right" side is always facing you.

ADDING A MOUTH

Thread your embroidery needle with a length of embroidery floss about 5-6 inches long.

1. Bring the needle from inside the piece to the outside, near the safety eye on your left. (photos 1+2)
2. Go across to the right side and insert the needle into the piece. Pull the needle through but make sure to not pull the floss all the way through. (photo 3)
3. Hold the thread in a smile shape and bring the needle through to the outside of the piece. You'll want to come out about one round down and in the center from where we first inserted the needle in step 1. (photos 4+5)

4. Pull the thread down to make a "V" shape. (photo 6)
5. Insert the needle very close to the spot where it just came out. You'll bring the needle around the main piece of floss making the smile and then insert it back into the piece. (photo 7)
6. Pull the thread through and make a knot to secure floss. (photo 8)

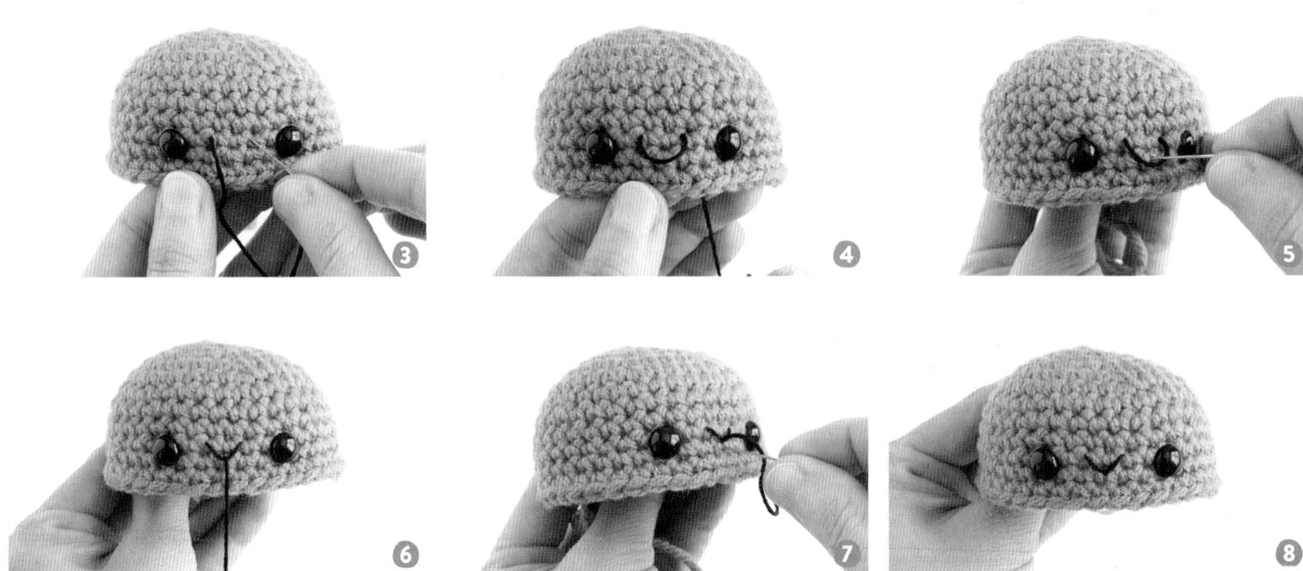

CLOSING UP YOUR PIECE

I like using this closing technique because it gives the piece a more finished look and the closure is nearly invisible.

1. When you've reached the end of the piece, cut the yarn and leave a tail for closing. Pull the yarn tail all the way through and pull to secure. (photos 1+2)
2. Thread the yarn tail onto the needle. Insert the needle into the front loop of the first stitch, working from the center to the outside. Pull the needle through. Continue going through the front loops of the remaining stitches. (photo 3)
3. Once you have reached the end, pull the yarn tail and the hole will close. (photos 4+5)
4. Insert the needle into the center of the hole and bring out on the side of the piece. Secure with a knot, trim tail and hide inside piece. (photos 6-8)

CLEAN FASTEN OFF

This is my favorite way to fasten off, as it gives you a clean edge and makes attaching the pieces much easier.

1. Once you reach the last stitch, cut the yarn and then pull the loop that was just on the hook all the way until the tail comes through. (photos 1-3)

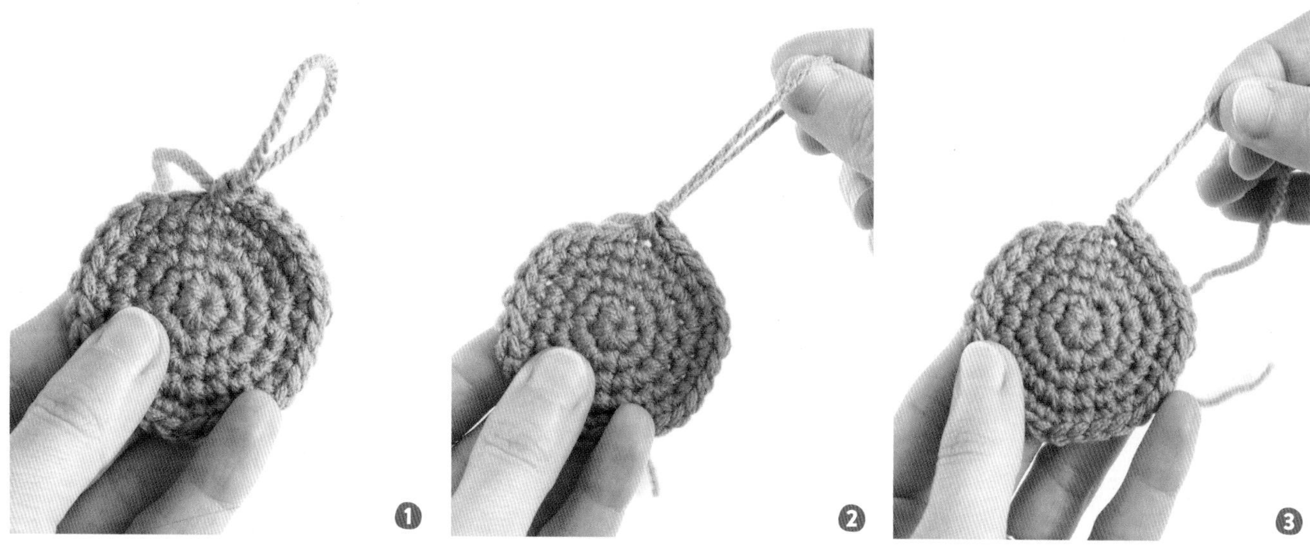

2. With a yarn needle, skip the first stitch of the round, the one directly next to our last stitch of the round, and go to the 2nd stitch.
3. Going from front to back, weave the needle under both loops (the "V"). Pull the yarn through. (photos 4+5)
4. Then weave the needle in between the "V" of the last stitch of the round, going from the front to the back. Only go under the back loop for this. (photo 6)
5. Pull the yarn through, making sure to not pull too tight. You'll notice that we just created a "stitch" and the fasten off is invisible. (photos 7-9)

Either weave in the tail or leave it for sewing, whichever the pattern states.

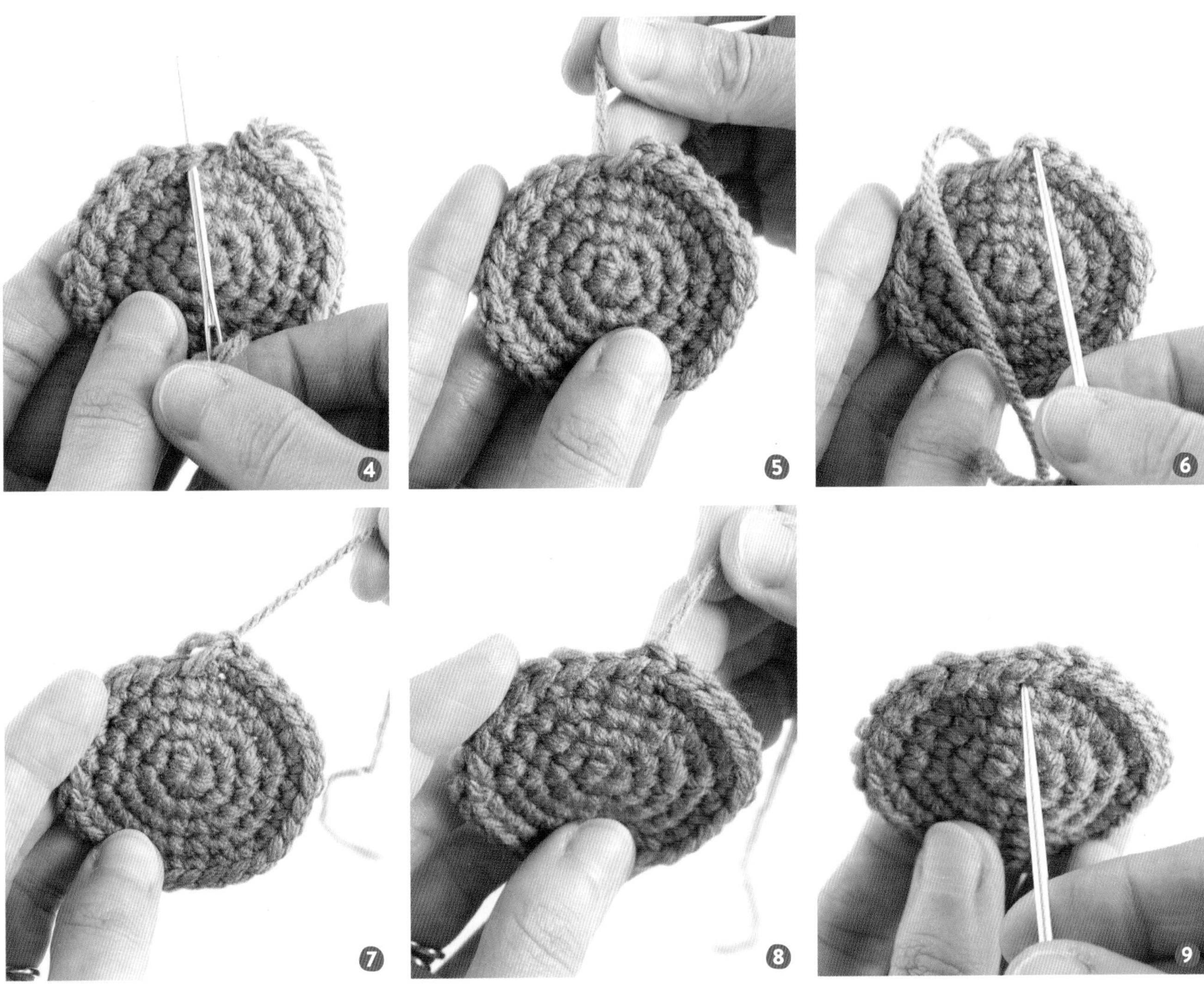

CROCHET TIPS

SKILL LEVELS

At the beginning of each pattern, you'll find the project skill level, which is indicated by a pair of scissors. One pair of scissors represents a beginner-friendly project, two pairs indicates an intermediate project, and three pairs indicates an expert project.

For beginners, I recommend flipping through the book and finding some of the easier projects to get started. If you have experience with crochet and are looking for more of a challenge, try out the expert patterns.

TIPS FOR READING A PATTERN

Most, if not all, of these patterns are crocheted in the round, or a continuous spiral. Do not join and chain after each round. Use a stitch marker to mark the last stitch in the round, moving it up as you complete each round.

When the number comes **AFTER** the stitch, such as ***Sc 3***, this means to place one single crochet into the next three stitches.

Example: *Sc 3, inc* 6 times. (30 sts)

You would make one single crochet into the next 3 stitches, then increase (inc) by placing 2 single crochets together into the next stitch. You will repeat this sequence 6 times and will end with 30 stitches in that round.

When the number comes **BEFORE** the stitch, such as ***3 Sc***, this means to place three single crochet stitches into the same stitch.

If you see, for example, "**R8-11**: Sc 36" this means you will continue crocheting 36 stitches total for rounds 8, 9, 10, and 11. I like to have a piece of paper and a pencil handy for keeping track of my rounds.

If there are two or more stitches listed in between commas, such as "Sc, **hdc dc**, sc", this means to place both an hdc and dc together in one stitch.

SAFARI

ELEPHANT

BEGINNER

FINISHED MEASUREMENTS

- Approx. 7 inches wide by 8 inches tall by 10 inches long

MATERIALS

- Worsted weight yarn: Gray and White
- Size F/3.75mm crochet hook
- One pair of 12mm safety eyes
- White felt
- Polyester fiberfill stuffing
- Yarn needle
- Scissors
- Stitch marker
- Straight pins
- Hot glue gun

ABBREVIATIONS

- BLO- Back Loops Only
- Inc- Increase
- Inv Dec- Invisible Decrease
- R- Round/Row
- Sc- Single Crochet
- St/s- Stitch/es

HEAD

Using gray yarn,

R1	6 sc in magic ring. (6 sts)
R2	Inc in each st around. (12 sts)
R3	*Sc 1, inc* 6 times. (18 sts)
R4	*Sc 2, inc* 6 times. (24 sts)
R5	*Sc 3, inc* 6 times. (30 sts)
R6	*Sc 4, inc* 6 times. (36 sts)
R7	*Sc 5, inc* 6 times. (42 sts)
R8	*Sc 6, inc* 6 times. (48 sts)
R9	*Sc 7, inc* 6 times. (54 sts)
R10-19	Sc 54.

Add the safety eyes between rounds 14 and 15, placing them 12 stitches apart.

R20	*Sc 7, inv dec* 6 times. (48 sts)
R21	*Sc 6, inv dec* 6 times. (42 sts)

Begin adding fiberfill and continue adding as you close the piece.

R22	*Sc 5, inv dec* 6 times. (36 sts)
R23	*Sc 4, inv dec* 6 times. (30 sts)
R24	*Sc 3, inv dec* 6 times. (24 sts)
R25	*Sc 2, inv dec* 6 times. (18 sts)
R26	*Sc 1, inv dec* 6 times. (12 sts)
R27	Inv dec around 6 times. (6 sts)

Fasten off and leave a long tail to close the piece and for sewing. (photo 1) The long tail will be used to sew the head to the body.

TRUNK

Using gray yarn,

R1	6 sc in magic ring. (6 sts)
R2	Inc in each st around. (12 sts)
R3	In BLO, Sc 12.
R4-6	Sc 12.
R7	Sc 2, inc, sc 5, inc, sc 3. (14 sts)
R8-12	Sc 14.
R13	Sc 3, inc, sc 6, inc, sc 3. (16 sts)
R14-16	Sc 16.

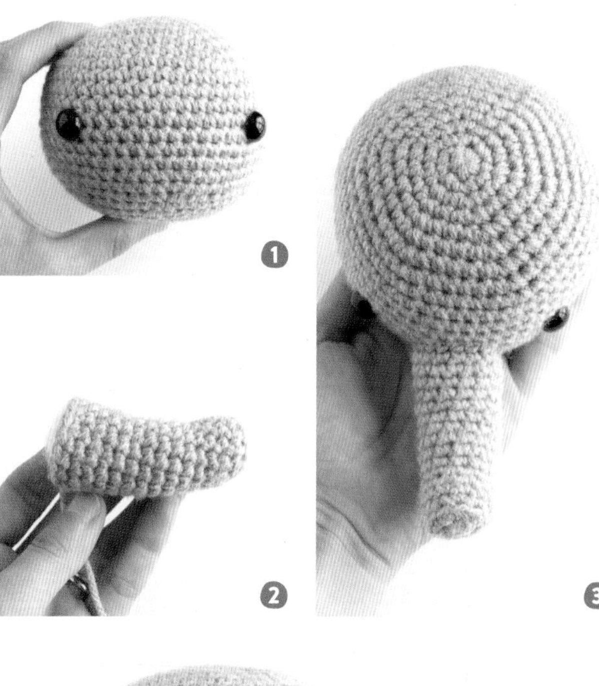

1 2 3

4

5

Fasten off and leave a tail for sewing. Add fiberfill to the trunk. (photo 2)

Using straight pins, pin the trunk between rounds 13-18 on the head. There will be 3 stitches on each side between the trunk and safety eyes. With the yarn needle and the tail, sew into place. Secure with a knot and hide inside the head. (photos 3-5)

TUSKS: MAKE 2

Using white yarn,

R1	6 sc in magic ring. (6 sts)
R2-8	Sc 6.

Fasten off and leave a tail for sewing. Leave tusks unstuffed. (photo 6)

Using straight pins, pin the tusks between rounds 16-18 on the head. Position them right along the edge of the trunk. With the yarn needle and the tail, sew into place. Secure with a knot and hide inside the head. (photos 7-9)

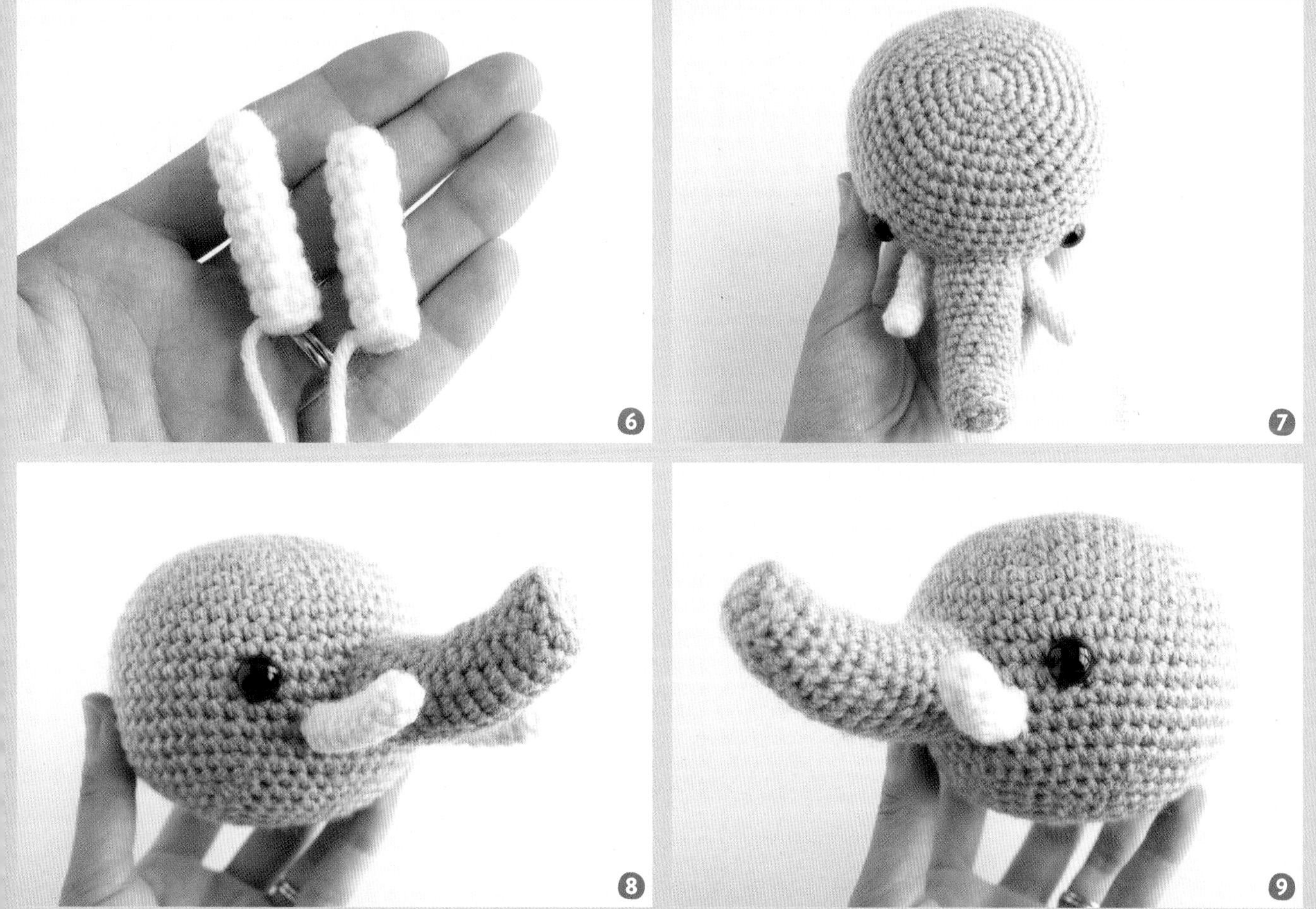

EARS: MAKE 2

Using gray yarn,

R1	6 sc in magic ring. (6 sts)
R2	Inc in each st around. (12 sts)
R3	*Sc 1, inc* 6 times. (18 sts)
R4	*Sc 2, inc* 6 times. (24 sts)
R5	*Sc 3, inc* 6 times. (30 sts)
R6	*Sc 4, inc* 6 times. (36 sts)
R7+8	Sc 36.
R9	*Sc 4, inv dec* 6 times. (30 sts)
R10	*Sc 3, inv dec* 6 times. (24 sts)
R11-13	Sc 24.
R14	*Sc 2, inv dec* 6 times. (18 sts)
R15-17	Sc 18.
R18	*Sc 1, inv dec* 6 times. (12 sts)
R19	Sc 12.
R20	Inv dec around 6 times. (6 sts)

Fasten off and leave a tail to close the piece. Leave ears unstuffed. (photos 10+11)

Cut two strands of gray yarn, both about 12 inches long, for sewing the ears to the head. Using straight pins, pin the ears between rounds 10-15 on both sides of the head, about 4 stitches away from the safety eyes. (photos 12-15) With the yarn needle and the tail, sew into place. Weave the needle into the head and then along the edge of the ear. (photos 16-20) Make sure to only sew rounds 9-13 of the ear to the head. (photos 21+22) This will make it so the ears hang off the head and look more natural. Secure with a knot and hide inside the head.

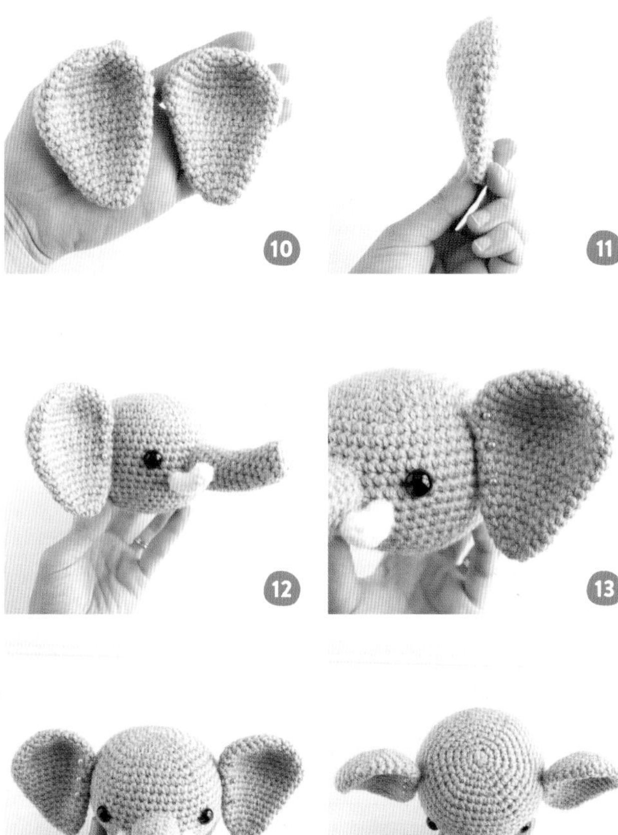

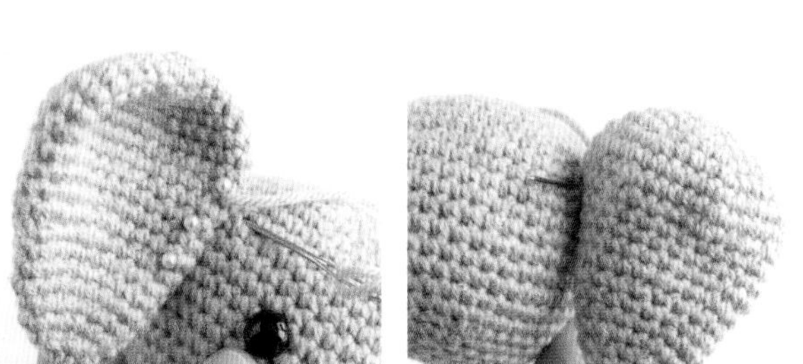

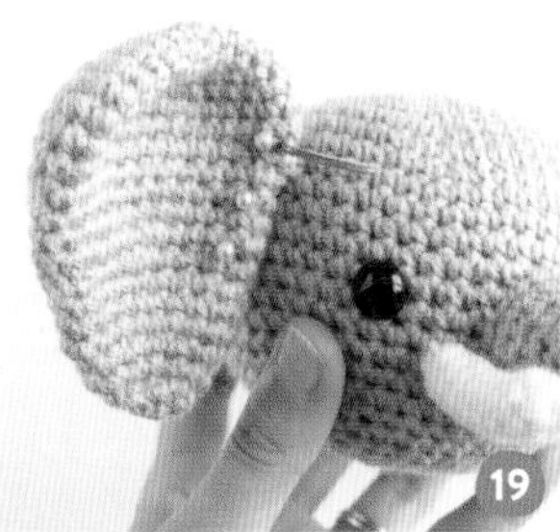

BODY

Using gray yarn,

R1	6 sc in magic ring. (6 sts)
R2	Inc in each st around. (12 sts)
R3	*Sc 1, inc* 6 times. (18 sts)
R4	*Sc 2, inc* 6 times. (24 sts)
R5	*Sc 3, inc* 6 times. (30 sts)
R6	*Sc 4, inc* 6 times. (36 sts)
R7	*Sc 5, inc* 6 times. (42 sts)
R8	*Sc 6, inc* 6 times. (48 sts)
R9-27	Sc 48.
R28	*Sc 6, inv dec* 6 times. (42 sts)
R29	*Sc 5, inv dec* 6 times. (36 sts)

Begin adding fiberfill and continue adding as you close the piece.

R30	*Sc 4, inv dec* 6 times. (30 sts)
R31	*Sc 3, inv dec* 6 times. (24 sts)
R32	*Sc 2, inv dec* 6 times. (18 sts)
R33	*Sc 1, inv dec* 6 times. (12 sts)
R34	Inv dec around 6 times. (6 sts)

Fasten off and leave a tail to close the piece. (photo 23)

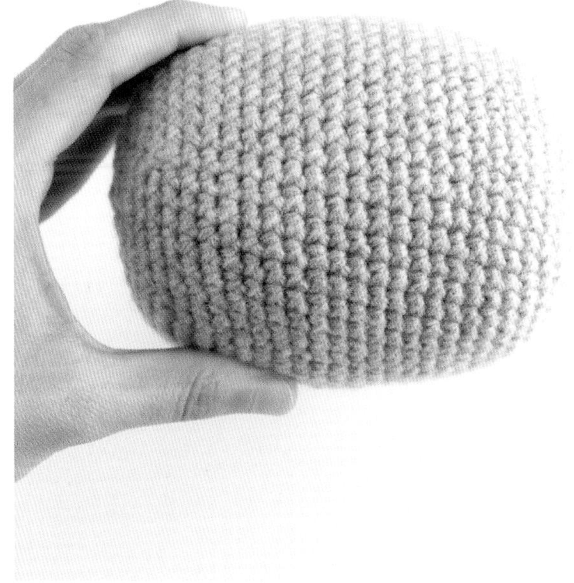

Using straight pins, pin the head to the body between rounds 5-12. (photos 24-26) It's important to place it between these rounds, as it will help balance the elephant and keep it on all four legs. Rounds 19-25 of the head will be sewn onto the body. Weave the yarn needle into the head and then into the body. (photos 27+28) If needed, sew around the head twice to make sure it is secure and not floppy. Secure with a knot and hide inside the body. (photos 29-32)

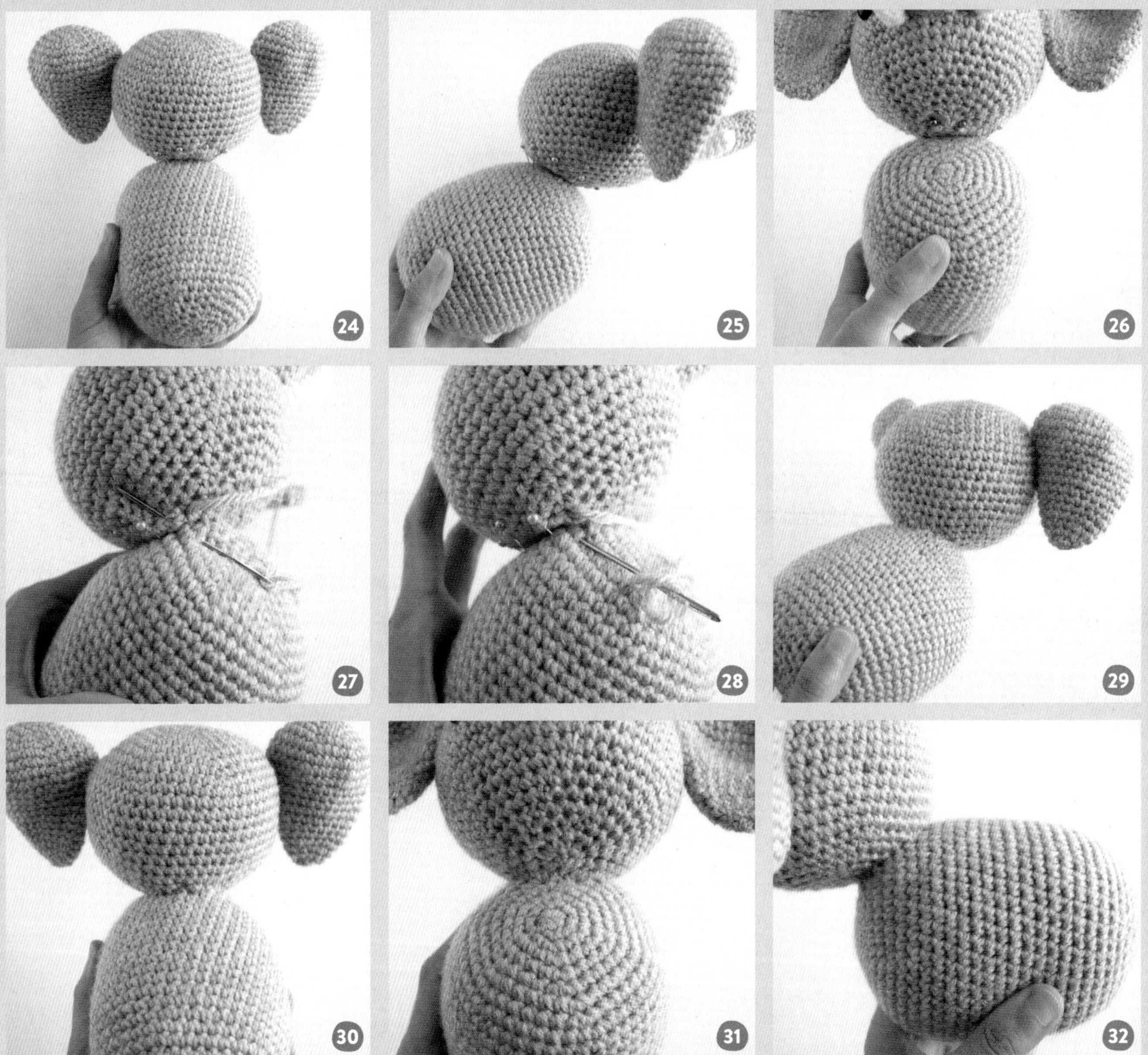

LEGS: MAKE 4

Using gray yarn,

R1	6 sc in magic ring. (6 sts)
R2	Inc in each st around. (12 sts)
R3	*Sc 1, inc* 6 times. (18 sts)
R4	In BLO, Sc 18.
R5-12	Sc 18.

Fasten off and leave a tail for sewing. Add fiberfill to the legs. (photo 33)

For the nails, draw out a nail on paper and then use it as a template for cutting out the nails. Each nail will have 3 bumps on top and a flat edge along the bottom. (photo 34) Line up the edge of the felt near the front loops left from R4. (photo 35) Use a hot glue gun to attach them to the legs.

Using straight pins, pin the legs to the body. Place the front legs between rounds 10-17 and use the yarn needle to sew into place. (photo 36) The front legs should be about 2 stitches apart from each other. Then place the back legs between rounds 24-30 and sew into place. (photos 37-39) The back legs should be about 3 stitches apart from each other. You'll want the back legs to go out slightly more than the front. This will help give the elephant more stability. Secure with a knot and hide inside the body. (photo 40)

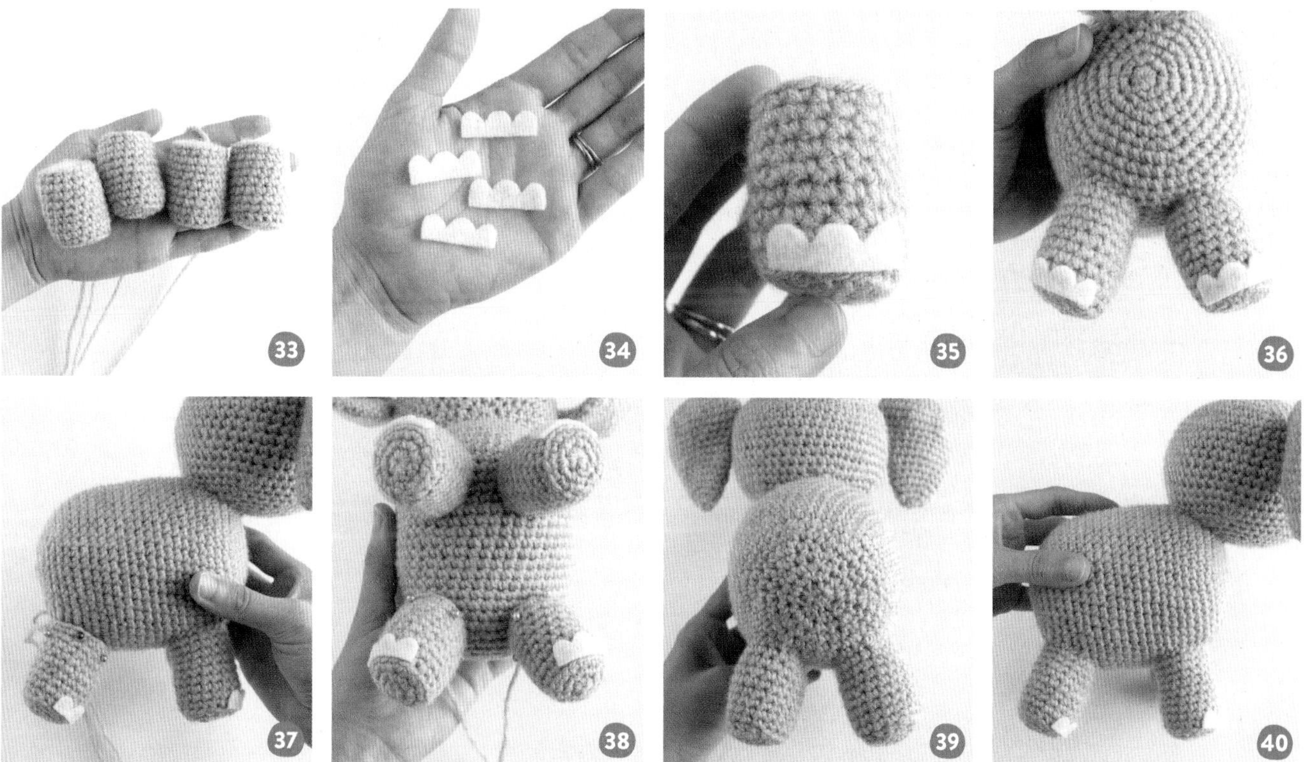

TAIL

Using gray yarn,

R1 6 sc in magic ring. (6 sts)

R2-9 Sc 6.

Fasten off and leave a tail for sewing. Leave the tail unstuffed. (photo 41)

To make the tail tuft, cut 1 strand, about 12 inches, of gray yarn. Tie a knot three times at one end. Then, using the yarn needle, weave through the opening of the tail and go through to the magic ring. (photo 42) Insert the needle into the center of the magic ring and pull the yarn through. (photos 43+44) Trim the yarn to about 1 inch. Do this two more times until you have three strands of gray yarn. (photo 45) Then, with the yarn needle, separate each strand so the hair becomes fluffy. (photos 46+47)

Using straight pins, pin the tail to the body near round 30. With the yarn needle and the tail, sew into place. Secure with a knot and hide inside the body. (photos 48+49)

41

42

43

44
45
46
47
48
49

GIRAFFE

BEGINNER

FINISHED MEASUREMENTS

- Approx. 4 inches wide by 10.5 inches tall by 6 inches long

MATERIALS

- Worsted weight yarn: Mustard Yellow, Tan, and Brown
- Size F/3.75mm crochet hook
- One pair of 10mm safety eyes
- Brown felt
- Polyester fiberfill stuffing
- Yarn needle
- Scissors
- Stitch marker
- Straight pins
- Hot glue gun

ABBREVIATIONS

- BLO- Back Loops Only
- Ch- Chain
- Dc- Double Crochet
- Hdc- Half Double Crochet
- Inc- Increase
- Inv Dec- Invisible Decrease
- R- Round/Row
- Sc- Single Crochet
- Sl St- Slip Stitch
- St/s- Stitch/es

HEAD

Using tan yarn,

R1	6 sc in magic ring. (6 sts)
R2	Inc in each st around. (12 sts)
R3	*Sc 1, inc* 6 times. (18 sts)
R4	*Sc 2, inc* 6 times. (24 sts)
R5	*Sc 3, inc* 6 times. (30 sts)
R6	*Sc 4, inc* 6 times. (36 sts)
R7+8	Sc 36.

Change to mustard yellow yarn,

R9-18	Sc 36.

Add the safety eyes between rounds 15 and 16, placing them 17 stitches apart.

R19	*Sc 4, inv dec* 6 times. (30 sts)
R20	*Sc 3, inv dec* 6 times. (24 sts)

Begin adding fiberfill and continue adding as you close the piece.

R21	*Sc 2, inv dec* 6 times. (18 sts)
R22	*Sc 1, inv dec* 6 times. (12 sts)
R23	Inv dec around 6 times. (6 sts)

Fasten off and leave a tail to close the piece. (photo 1)

EARS: MAKE 2

Using mustard yellow yarn,

R1	6 sc in magic ring. (6 sts)
R2	Sc 6.
R3	*Sc 1, inc* 3 times. (9 sts)
R4	*Sc 2, inc* 3 times. (12 sts)
R5	*Sc 3, inc* 3 times. (15 sts)
R6	*Sc 4, inc* 3 times. (18 sts)
R7+8	Sc 18.
R9	*Sc 4, inv dec* 3 times. (15 sts)
R10	*Sc 3, inv dec* 3 times. (12 sts)
R11	*Sc 2, inv dec* 3 times. (9 sts)

Fasten off and leave a tail for sewing. Leave the ears unstuffed. (photo 2)

Using straight pins, pin the ears between rounds 19 and 20 on both sides of the head, about 10 stitches apart. (photos 3-6) With the yarn needle and the tail, sew into place. Secure with a knot and hide inside the head.

OSSICONES: MAKE 2

Using brown yarn,

R1 6 sc in magic ring. (6 sts)

R2 Inc in each st around. (12 sts)

R3 Sc 12.

R4 *Sc 1, inv dec* 4 times. (8 sts) (photo 7)

Change to mustard yellow yarn, (photo 8)

R5 *Sc 2, inv dec* 2 times. (6 sts) (photo 9)

Add a little bit of fiberfill to the brown ball part only. The rest will remain unstuffed.

R6-9 Sc 6.

Fasten off and leave a tail for sewing. (photo 10)

Using straight pins, pin the ossicones between rounds 19 and 20 on both sides of the head, about 2 stitches apart. These will go right between the ears. (photos 11+12) With the yarn needle and the tail, sew into place. Secure with a knot and hide inside the head. (photos 13+14)

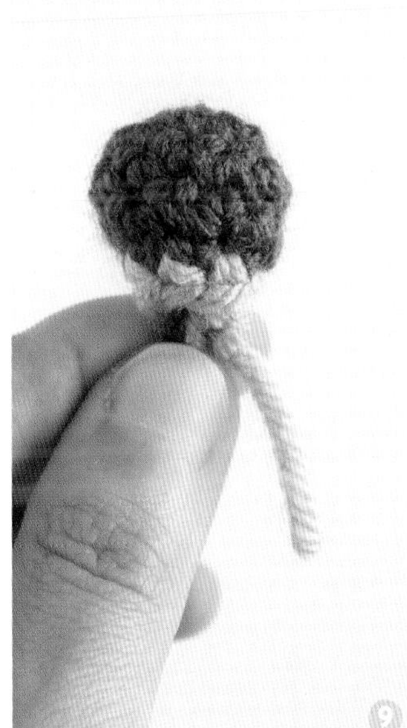

NECK

Using mustard yellow yarn,

Leave about 12 inches at the beginning for sewing.

R1 Ch 18 then in the 1st ch, insert the hook into the top loop and make a sc. This will join the piece to form a circle. (photos 15-17) Place a stitch marker in this sc, as it will mark the END of the round. (photo 18) Then, in both loops, leaving the back "bump", sc around the chain. (18 sts) (photos 19-21) Pull the tail left at the beginning through the circle. (photo 22)

R2-11 Sc 18.

Fasten off and leave a tail for sewing. (photo 23)

Using straight pins, pin the neck between rounds 12-18 on the head. (photos 24+25) Use the tail left at the end to sew the neck to the head. Weave the needle through the head and then under both loops (the "V") of the stitches from R11 of the neck. (photo 26) Secure with a knot and hide inside the head. (photos 27-29) The tail left at the beginning will be used to sew the neck to the body. Add fiberfill to the neck.

21
22
23
24
25
26
27
28
29

BODY

Using mustard yellow yarn,

R1	6 sc in magic ring. (6 sts)
R2	Inc in each st around. (12 sts)
R3	*Sc 1, inc* 6 times. (18 sts)
R4	*Sc 2, inc* 6 times. (24 sts)
R5	*Sc 3, inc* 6 times. (30 sts)
R6	*Sc 4, inc* 6 times. (36 sts)
R7	*Sc 5, inc* 6 times. (42 sts)
R8-23	Sc 42.
R24	*Sc 5, inv dec* 6 times. (36 sts)
R25	*Sc 4, inv dec* 6 times. (30 sts)
R26	*Sc 3, inv dec* 6 times. (24 sts)

Begin adding fiberfill and continue adding as you close the piece.

R27	*Sc 2, inv dec* 6 times. (18 sts)
R28	*Sc 1, inv dec* 6 times. (12 sts)
R29	Inv dec around 6 times. (6 sts)

Fasten off and leave a tail to close the piece. (photo 30)

Using straight pins, pin the neck between rounds 7-14 on the body. (photos 31+32) Use the tail left at the beginning of the neck pattern to sew the neck to the body. Weave the needle through the body and then through the back "bumps" left over from R1 of the neck. (photo 33) Add more fiberfill if needed before closing the piece. Secure with a knot and hide inside the body.

LEGS: MAKE 4

Using brown yarn,

R1	6 sc in magic ring. (6 sts)
R2	Inc in each st around. (12 sts)
R3	*Sc 1, inc* 6 times. (18 sts)
R4	In BLO, Sc 18.
R5	Sc 18.

Change to mustard yellow yarn, (photos 34-36)

R6-14	Sc 18.

Fasten off and leave a tail for sewing. Add fiberfill to the legs. (photo 37)

Using straight pins, pin the legs to the body. Place the front legs between rounds 8-15 and use the yarn needle to sew into place. (photos 38+39) Then place the back legs between rounds 19-25 and sew into place. (photos 40+41) Both sets of legs will be close together. Secure with a knot and hide inside the body. (photo 42)

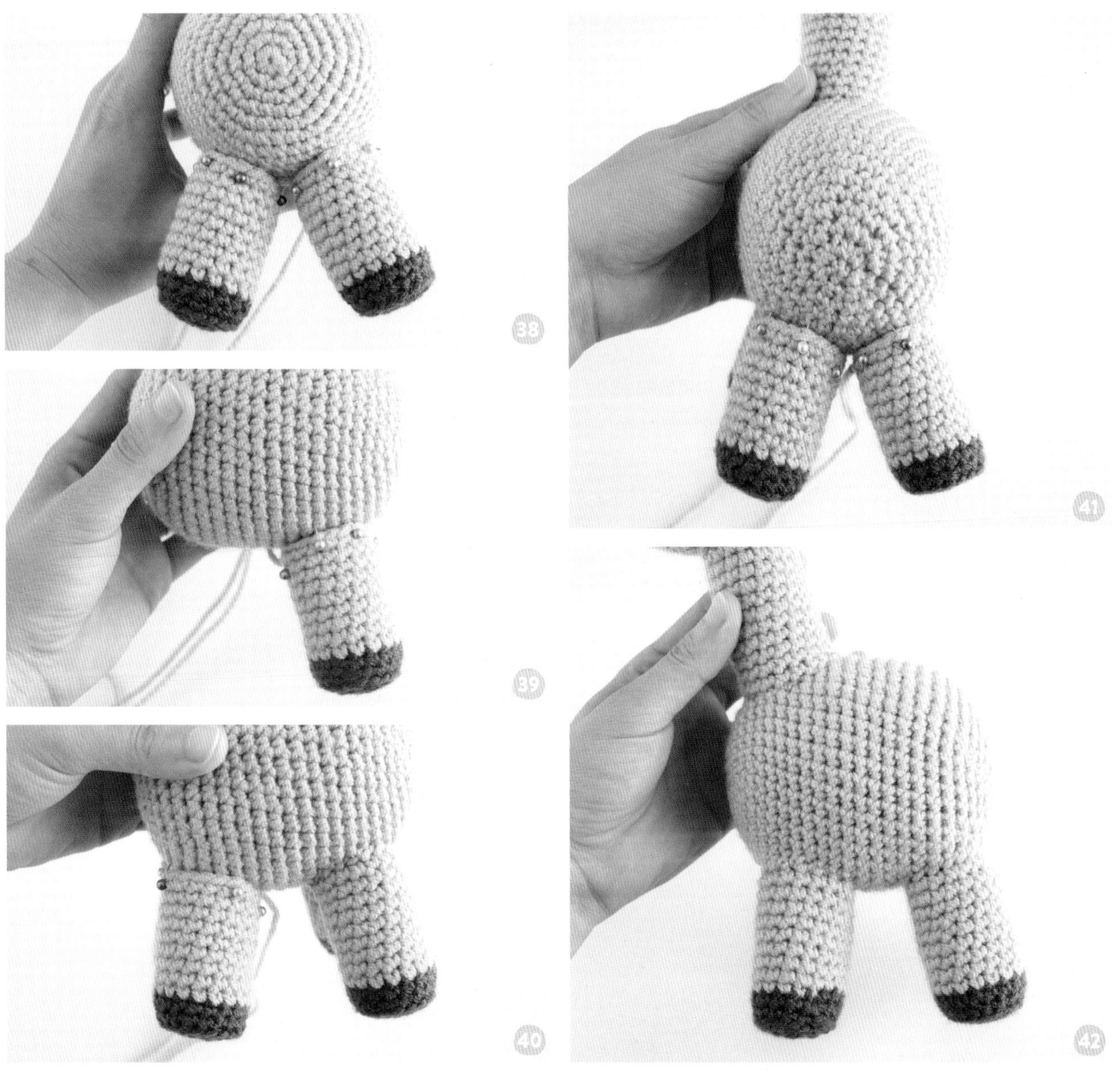

38

39

40

41

42

TAIL

Using mustard yellow yarn,

R1	6 sc in magic ring. (6 sts)
R2-10	Sc 6.

Fasten off and leave a tail for closing the piece and sewing. Leave the tail unstuffed. (photo 43)

To make the tail tuft, cut 1 strand, about 12 inches, of brown yarn. Tie a knot three times at one end. Then, using the yarn needle, weave through the opening of the tail and go through to the magic ring. (photo 44) Insert the needle into the center of the magic ring and pull the yarn through. (photos 45+46) Trim the yarn to about 1 inch. Do this two more times until you have three strands of brown yarn. (photo 47) Then, with the yarn needle, separate each strand so the hair becomes fluffy. (photos 48+49)

Using straight pins, pin the tail to the body near round 25. (photo 50) With the yarn needle and the tail, sew into place. Secure with a knot and hide inside the body. (photo 51)

43

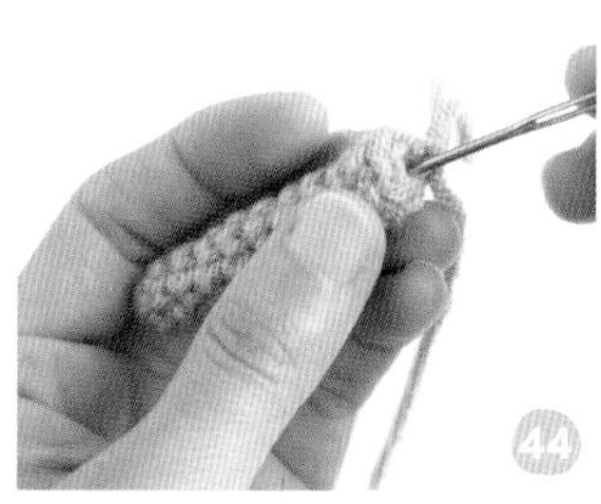
44

45

46

48

49

50

51

47

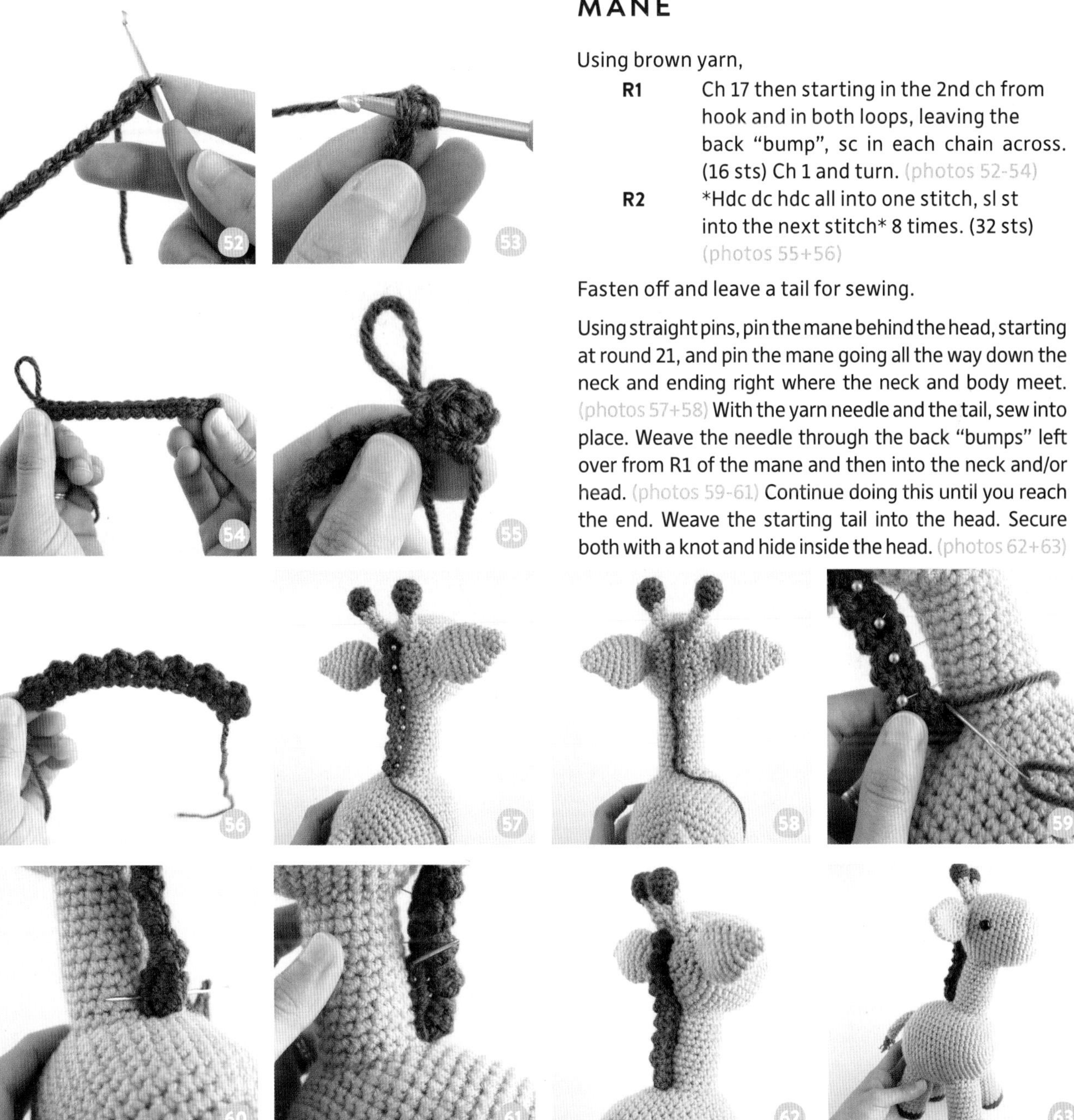

MANE

Using brown yarn,

R1 Ch 17 then starting in the 2nd ch from hook and in both loops, leaving the back "bump", sc in each chain across. (16 sts) Ch 1 and turn. (photos 52-54)

R2 *Hdc dc hdc all into one stitch, sl st into the next stitch* 8 times. (32 sts) (photos 55+56)

Fasten off and leave a tail for sewing.

Using straight pins, pin the mane behind the head, starting at round 21, and pin the mane going all the way down the neck and ending right where the neck and body meet. (photos 57+58) With the yarn needle and the tail, sew into place. Weave the needle through the back "bumps" left over from R1 of the mane and then into the neck and/or head. (photos 59-61) Continue doing this until you reach the end. Weave the starting tail into the head. Secure both with a knot and hide inside the head. (photos 62+63)

SPOTS

For the spots, take brown felt and cut out 9 different size "blobs". Cut out 2 large, 5 medium/small, and 2 extra small. You can add more spots if you'd like! (photo 64) You'll want each of these to be different since the spots on a giraffe are never the same. I cut mine so that when placed together, they looked as if they could fit together like a puzzle piece.

Next, take straight pins and position the spots where you'd like on the body. I placed the two large spots on either side of the body and then spread out the other sizes where I thought they fit. (photos 65-67) Use hot glue to glue the spots into place. (photos 68-70)

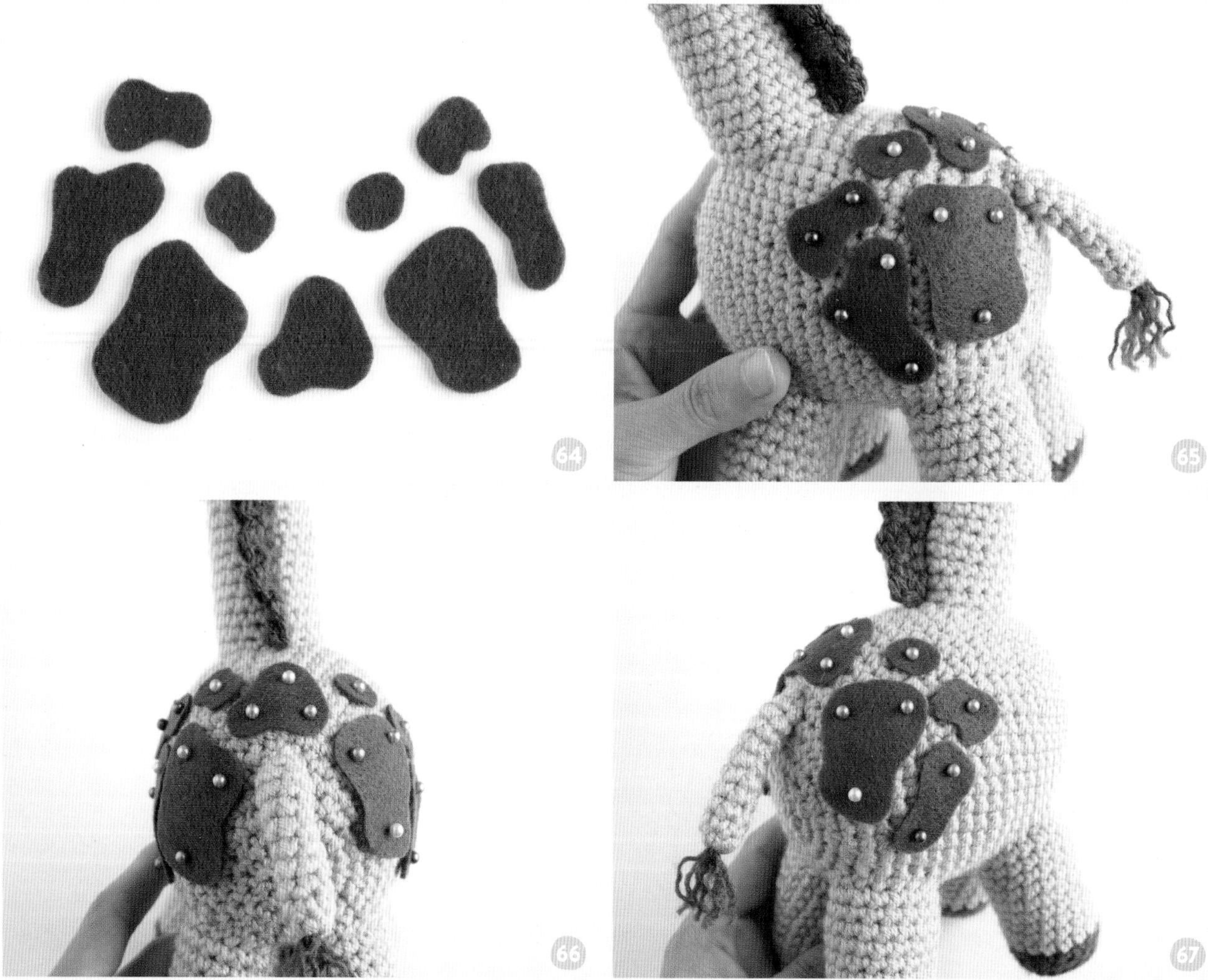

68

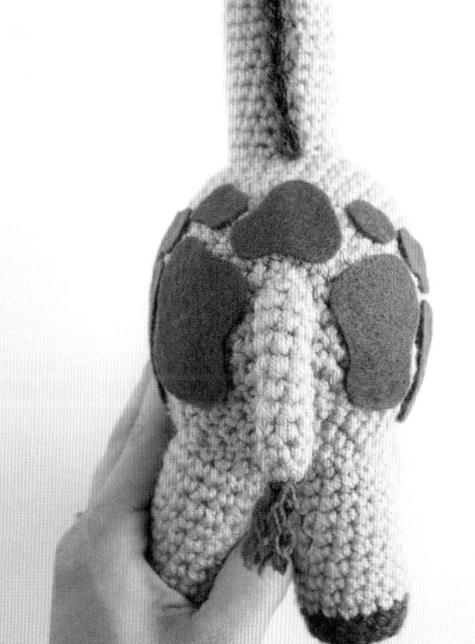
69

70

HIPPO

BEGINNER

FINISHED MEASUREMENTS

- Approx. 5 inches wide by 7 inches tall by 10 inches long

MATERIALS

- Worsted weight yarn: Purple and Dark Purple
- Size F/3.75mm crochet hook
- One pair of 10mm safety eyes
- Tan felt
- Polyester fiberfill stuffing
- Yarn needle
- Scissors
- Stitch marker
- Straight pins
- Hot glue gun

ABBREVIATIONS

- BLO- Back Loops Only
- Ch- Chain
- FLO- Front Loops Only
- Inc- Increase
- Inv Dec- Invisible Decrease
- R- Round/Row
- Sc- Single Crochet
- St/s- Stitch/es

HEAD

Using purple yarn,

R1	Ch 11 then starting in the 2nd ch from the hook and in both loops, leaving the back "bump", sc in each chain across 10 times. (photos 1-3) Then turn the work and sc across the back "bumps" 10 times. (20 sts) (photos 4-6)
R2	Inc, sc 8, inc in the next two sts, sc 8, inc. (24 sts) (photos 7+8)
R3	*Sc 3, inc* 6 times. (30 sts)
R4	*Sc 4, inc* 6 times. (36 sts)
R5-9	Sc 36. (photos 9-11)

Make the nostrils using dark purple yarn. Use about a 15-inch-long piece of the yarn. An easy way to find where you want the nostrils is to use straight pins. Place 4 straight pins (2 for each nostril) between rounds 4 and 5. Each nostril will be 3 stitches in length and there will be 5 stitches in between each one. (photo 12) Weave the needle over the spot about 5 to 6 times to build up the nostril. (photos 13+14) Secure the dark purple yarn with a knot. (photos 15+16)

R10	*Sc 4, inv dec* 6 times. (30 sts) (photo 17)
R11	Sc 30.
R12	In FLO, Sc 30. (photos 18-20)
R13	*Sc 4, inc* 6 times. (36 sts)
R14	*Sc 5, inc* 6 times. (42 sts)
R15	*Sc 6, inc* 6 times. (48 sts)
R16	*Sc 7, inc* 6 times. (54 sts)
R17-25	Sc 54.

Add the safety eyes between rounds 17 and 18, placing them about 24 stitches apart.

Add fiberfill to the nose and then continue adding as you begin to close the piece.

R26	*Sc 7, inv dec* 6 times. (48 sts)
R27	*Sc 6, inv dec* 6 times. (42 sts)
R28	*Sc 5, inv dec* 6 times. (36 sts)
R29	*Sc 4, inv dec* 6 times. (30 sts)
R30	*Sc 3, inv dec* 6 times. (24 sts)
R31	*Sc 2, inv dec* 6 times. (18 sts)

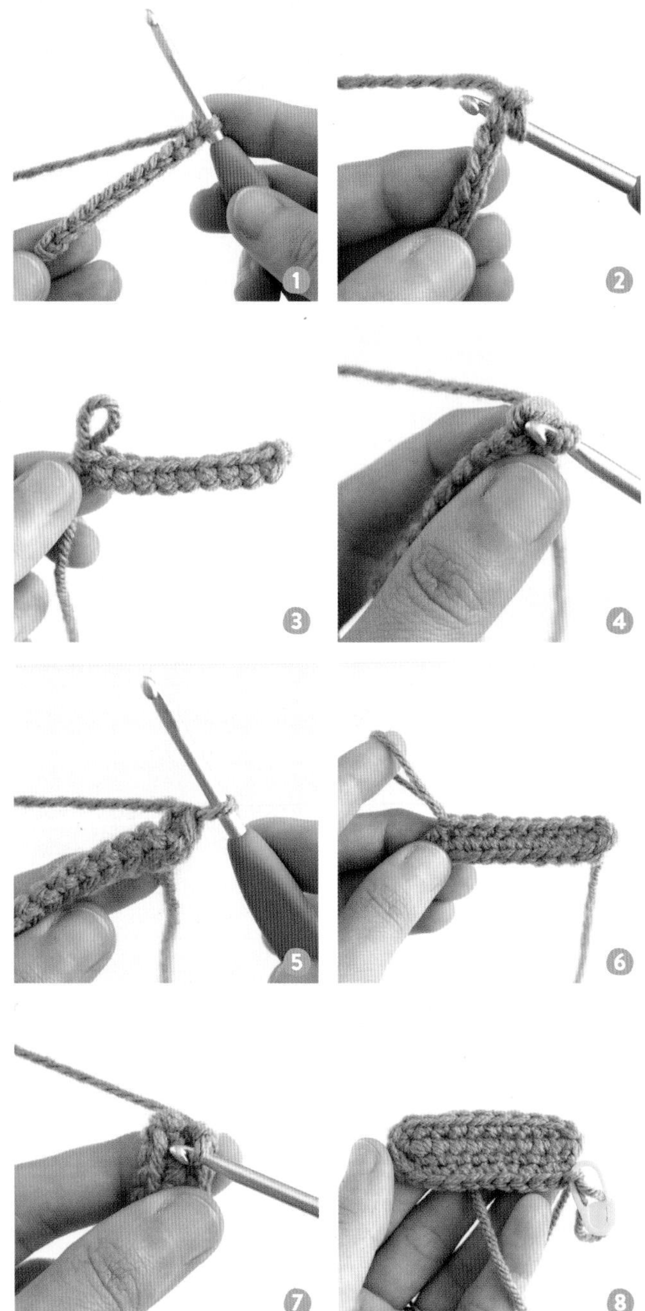

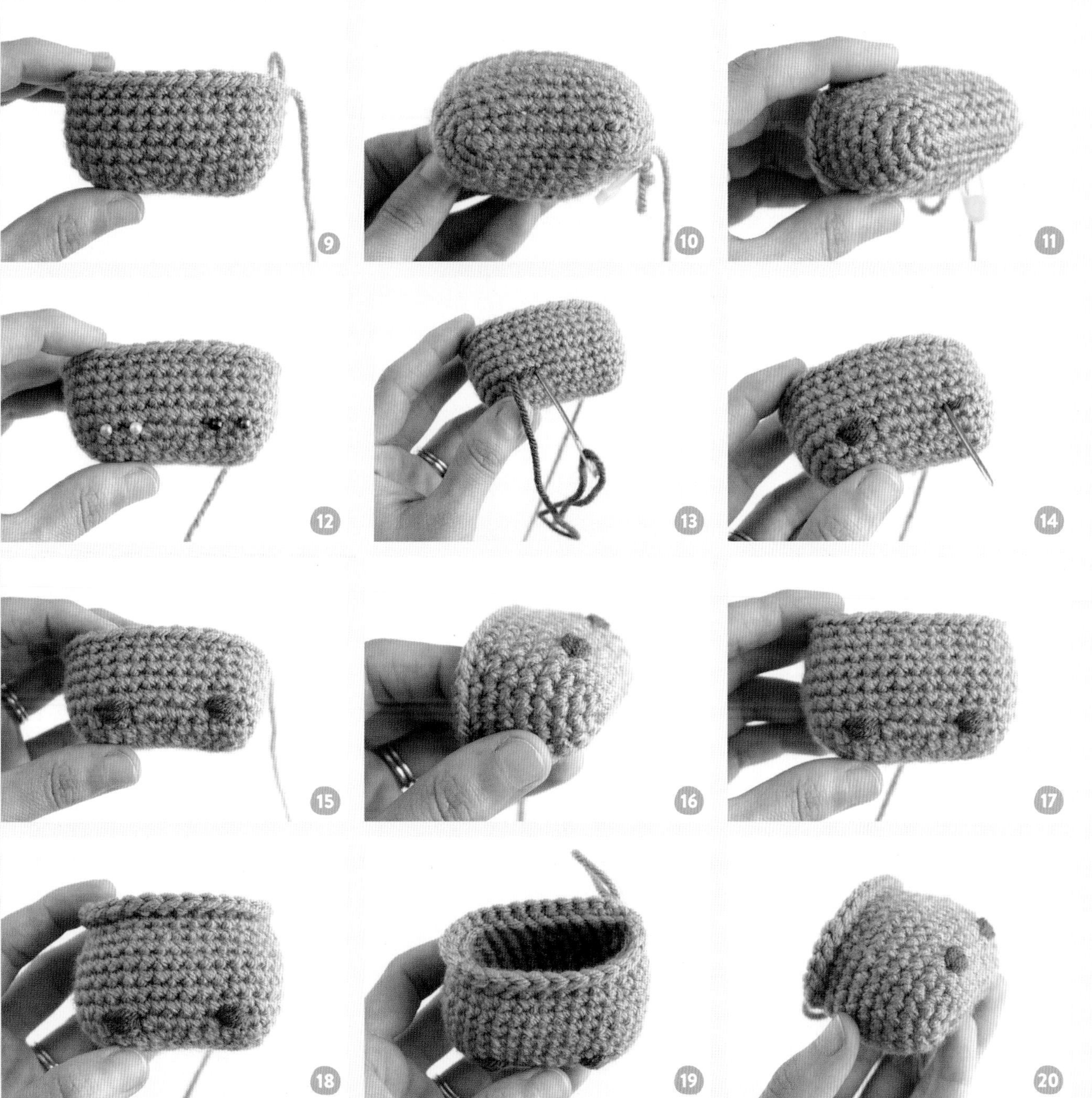

R32	*Sc 1, inv dec* 6 times. (12 sts)
R33	Inv dec around 6 times. (6 sts)

Fasten off and leave a long tail to close the piece and for sewing. (photos 21-23) The long tail will be used to sew the head to the body.

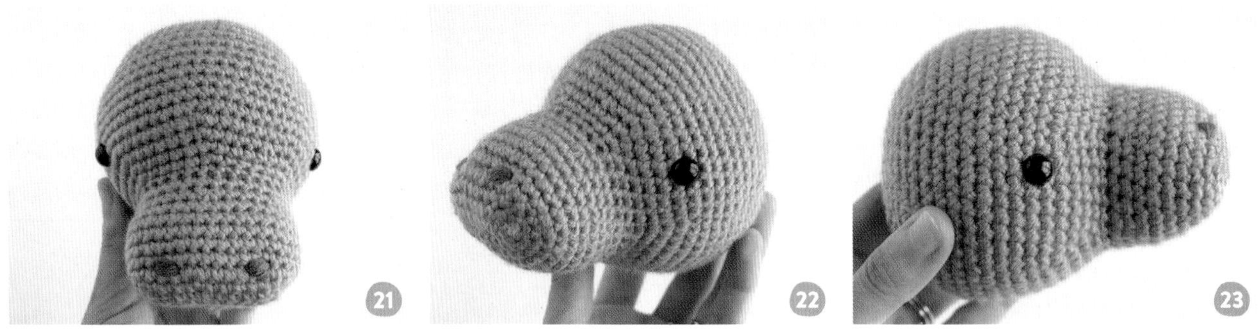

EARS: MAKE 2

Using purple yarn,

R1	6 sc in magic ring. (6 sts)
R2	Inc in each st around. (12 sts)
R3	*Sc 1, inc* 6 times. (18 sts)
R4	*Sc 1, inv dec* 6 times. (12 sts)
R5-7	Sc 12.
R8	*Sc 1, inv dec* 4 times. (8 sts)

Fasten off and leave a tail for sewing. Leave the ears unstuffed. (photo 24)

Pinch round 8 of the ears together. (photo 25) With the yarn needle and the tail, sew the pinched area together. (photos 26-29) Then using straight pins, pin the ears between rounds 23-25, placing them about 15 stitches apart. With the yarn needle and the tail, sew into place. Secure with a knot and hide inside the head. (photos 30+31)

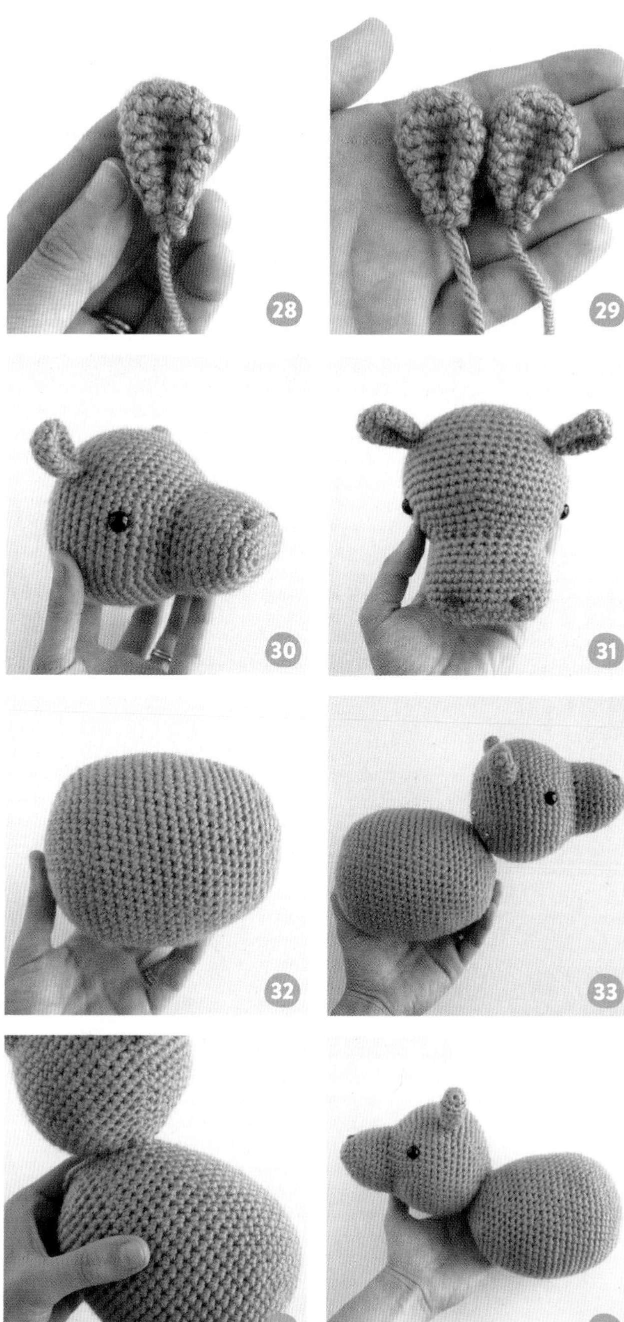

BODY

Using purple yarn,

R1	6 sc in magic ring. (6 sts)
R2	Inc in each st around. (12 sts)
R3	*Sc 1, inc* 6 times. (18 sts)
R4	*Sc 2, inc* 6 times. (24 sts)
R5	*Sc 3, inc* 6 times. (30 sts)
R6	*Sc 4, inc* 6 times. (36 sts)
R7	*Sc 5, inc* 6 times. (42 sts)
R8	*Sc 6, inc* 6 times. (48 sts)
R9	*Sc 7, inc* 6 times. (54 sts)
R10-22	Sc 54.
R23	*Sc 7, inv dec* 6 times. (48 sts)
R24-27	Sc 48.
R28	*Sc 6, inv dec* 6 times. (42 sts)
R29	Sc 42.
R30	*Sc 5, inv dec* 6 times. (36 sts)
R31	Sc 36.

Begin adding fiberfill and continue adding as you close the piece.

R32	*Sc 4, inv dec* 6 times. (30 sts)
R33	Sc 30.
R34	*Sc 3, inv dec* 6 times. (24 sts)
R35	*Sc 2, inv dec* 6 times. (18 sts)
R36	*Sc 1, inv dec* 6 times. (12 sts)
R37	Inv dec around 6 times. (6 sts)

Fasten off and leave a tail to close the piece. (photo 32)

Using straight pins, pin the head to the body between rounds 30-36. (photo 33) It's important to place it between these rounds, as it will help balance the hippo and keep it on all four legs. Rounds 26-31 of the head will be sewn onto the body. With the yarn needle and the tail, weave into the head and then into the body. (photo 34) If needed, sew around the head twice to make sure it is secure and not floppy. Secure with a knot and hide inside the body. (photo 35)

LEGS: MAKE 4

Using dark purple yarn,

R1	6 sc in magic ring. (6 sts)
R2	Inc in each st around. (12 sts)
R3	*Sc 1, inc* 6 times. (18 sts)

Change to purple yarn, (photos 36+37)

R4	In BLO, Sc 18. (photo 38)
R5-10	Sc 18.

Fasten off and leave a tail for sewing. Add fiberfill to the legs. (photo 39)

Using straight pins, pin the legs to the body. Place the front legs between rounds 23-30 and use the yarn needle to sew into place. (photo 40) The front legs should be about 3 stitches apart from each other. Then place the back legs between rounds 9-16. (photo 41) The back legs should be about 5 stitches apart from each other. You'll want the back legs to go out slightly more than the front. This will help give the hippo some stability. With the yarn needle and the tail, sew into place. Secure with a knot and hide inside the body. (photos 42+43)

For the nails, draw out a nail on paper and then use it as a template for cutting out the nails. Each nail will have 3 small bumps on the top and a flat edge along the bottom. (photo 44) Line up the edge of the felt near the front loops left from R4. (photo 45) Use a hot glue gun to attach them to the legs. (photo 46)

TAIL

Using purple yarn,

R1	6 sc in magic ring. (6 sts)
R2	Sc 6.
R3	*Sc 1, inc* 3 times. (9 sts)
R4	Sc 9.
R5	*Sc 2, inc* 3 times. (12 sts)
R6	Sc 12.
R7	*Sc 2, inv dec* 3 times. (9 sts)

Fasten off and leave a tail for sewing. Add a little bit of fiberfill to the tail. (photo 47)

Using straight pins, pin the tail in place on the body between rounds 5-7. (photo 48) With the yarn needle and the tail, sew into place. Secure with a knot and hide inside the body. (photos 49-51)

LION

INTERMEDIATE

FINISHED MEASUREMENTS

- Approx. 5.5 inches wide by 7.5 inches tall

MATERIALS

- Worsted weight yarn: Speckled Mustard Yellow, Cream, Tan, and Gold
- Size F/3.75mm crochet hook
- One pair of 10mm safety eyes
- Brown embroidery floss and needle
- Polyester fiberfill stuffing
- Yarn needle
- Scissors
- Stitch marker
- Straight pins
- Optional: Pet slicker brush

ABBREVIATIONS

- Ch- Chain
- Dc Inc- Double Crochet Increase
- Inc- Increase
- Inv Dec- Invisible Decrease
- R- Round/Row
- Sc- Single Crochet
- St/s- Stitch/es
- Tr Inc- Treble Crochet Increase

HEAD

Using mustard yellow yarn,

R1 6 sc in magic ring. (6 sts)
R2 Inc in each st around. (12 sts)
R3 *Sc 1, inc* 6 times. (18 sts)
R4 *Sc 2, inc* 6 times. (24 sts)
R5 *Sc 3, inc* 6 times. (30 sts)
R6 *Sc 4, inc* 6 times. (36 sts)
R7 *Sc 5, inc* 6 times. (42 sts)
R8 *Sc 6, inc* 6 times. (48 sts)
R9-17 Sc 48.

Add the safety eyes between rounds 13 and 14, placing them 8 stitches apart.

With brown embroidery floss, sew on the nose. Start just below round 12 and stitch completely over round 13. (photo 1) Next, make one vertical line coming up from round 15 and meeting with the bottom center of the nose. (photo 2) Then, make two angled lines on round 16. These will both meet at the point of the center line. (photo 3) Finally, on the angled lines we just created, make another angled line, this time going in the opposite direction and meeting at the point of the first angled line (where rounds 16 and 17 meet). This will create a "V" shape. (photo 4)

R18 *Sc 6, inv dec* 6 times. (42 sts)
R19 *Sc 5, inv dec* 6 times. (36 sts)

Begin adding fiberfill and continue adding as you close the piece.

R20 *Sc 4, inv dec* 6 times. (30 sts)
R21 *Sc 3, inv dec* 6 times. (24 sts)
R22 *Sc 2, inv dec* 6 times. (18 sts)
R23 *Sc 1, inv dec* 6 times. (12 sts)
R24 Inv dec around 6 times. (6 sts)

Fasten off and leave a long tail to close the piece and for sewing. (photo 5) The long tail will be used to sew the head to the body.

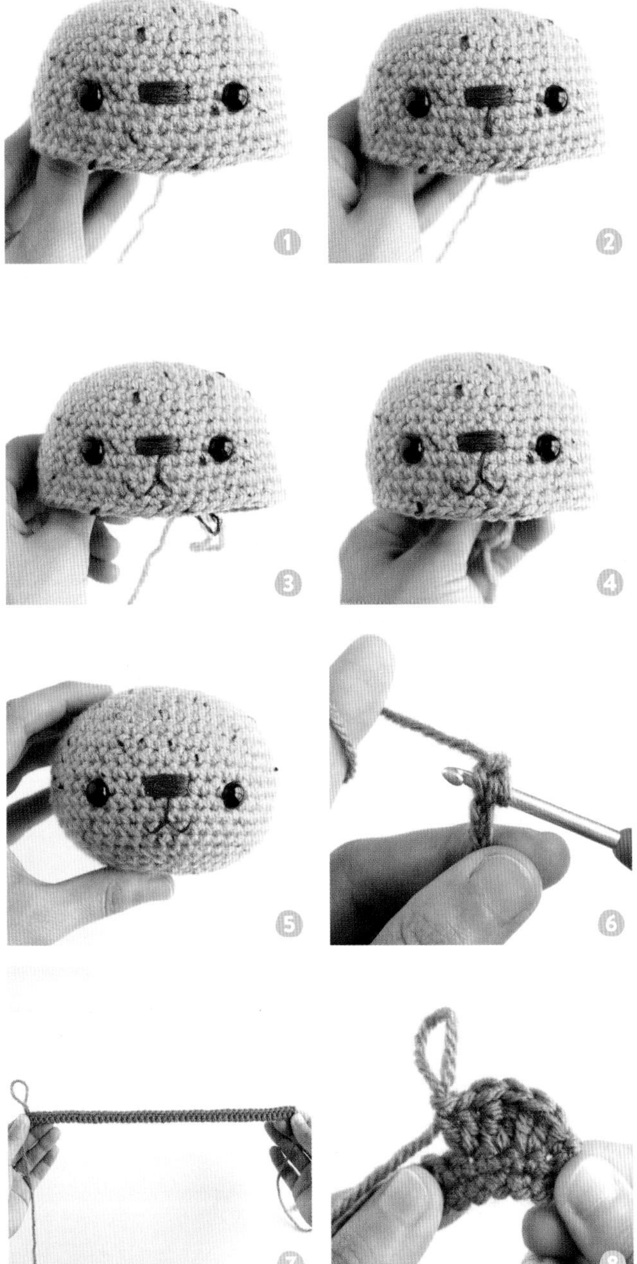

MANE

Using gold yarn,

R1	Ch 50 then starting in the 2nd ch from the hook and in both loops, leaving the back "bump", sc in each chain across. (49 sts) Ch 1 and turn. (photo 6)
R2	Sc 49. Ch 1 and turn. (photo 7)
R3	* Sc, dc inc, tr inc, dc inc* 12 times, sc in the last st. (85 sts) (photo 8)

9 10 11 12 13 14 15 16 17 18

19

Fasten off and leave an extra-long tail for sewing. (photo 9) Position the mane evenly around the head, starting at the center of the magic ring. (photo 10) The ends of the mane should meet up right at round 24 of the head. Using straight pins, pin the mane to the head. (photo 11) With the yarn needle and the long tail, sew the two ends of the mane together. (photos 12+13) Weave the needle through these edges until you reach where the mane and head meet. Next, weave the yarn needle through the back "bumps" left over from R1 of the mane and then into the head. (photos 14-16) Continue sewing all the way around. Make sure to weave the starting tail into the head. Secure both tails with a knot and hide inside the head. (photos 17-19)

FACE PIECE

Using cream yarn,

R1	Ch 5 then starting in the 2nd ch from the hook and in both loops, leaving the back "bump", sc in each chain across. (4 sts) Ch 1 and turn. (photos 20-22)
R2	Inc, sc 2, inc. (6 sts) Ch 1 and turn.
R3	Sc 6. Ch 1 and turn.
R4	Inc, sc 4, inc. (8 sts) Ch 1 and turn.
R5	Sc 8. Ch 1 and turn.
R6	Inc, sc 6, inc. (10 sts) Ch 1 and turn.
R7-9	Sc 10. Ch 1 and turn after each row, except for row 9. (photo 23)

For this next row we are going to work around the edge of the piece.

R10	Sc in the same space as the last sc, then continue single crocheting around the three edges, stopping right before round 9. (30 sts, including the 10 sts from R9 that were unworked) (photos 24-26)

Fasten off and leave a long tail for sewing.

Using straight pins, pin the face piece to the head, starting at the magic ring and ending near round 9. (photo 27) With the yarn needle and the tail, sew the piece to the head. Weave the needle under both loops (the "V") from the stitches on R10 of the face piece and then into the head, coming out through one of the stitch holes. (photo 28) Insert the needle into the same stitch hole and then go over to the next stitch on the face piece and repeat. (photo 29) Make sure to go under the stitches and not over them to create a clean finish. Secure with a knot and hide inside the head. (photo 30)

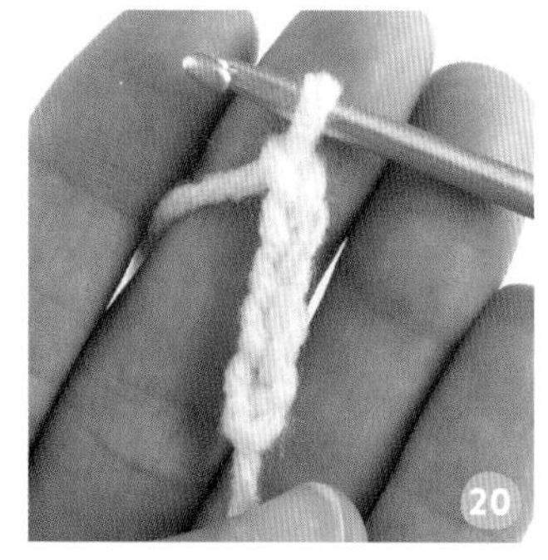
20

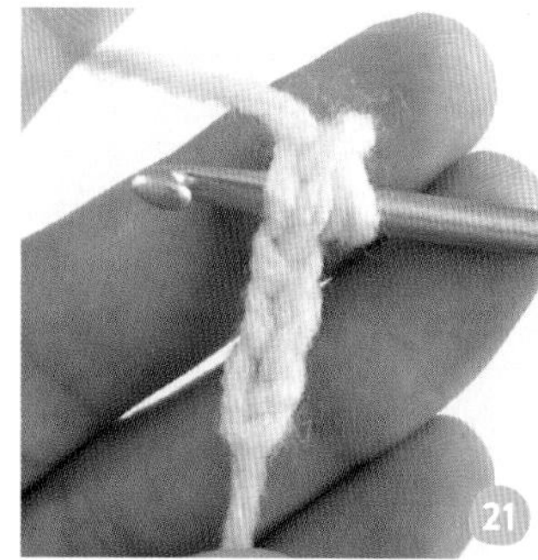
21

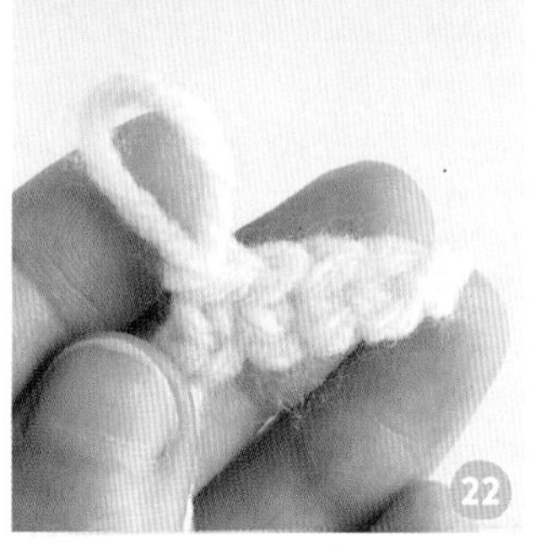
22

23

24

25

26

27

EARS: MAKE 2

Using mustard yellow yarn,

R1 8 sc in magic ring. (8 sts) Ch 1 and turn. (photos 31+32)

R2 Inc in each st around. (16 sts) (photo 33)

Fasten off and leave a tail for sewing. (photo 34)

Using straight pins, pin the ears between rounds 6-10 on each side of the face piece. (photo 35) The edge will touch the face piece. With the yarn needle and the tail, sew the ears to the head. (photo 36) Secure with a knot and hide inside the body.

BODY

Using mustard yellow yarn,

R1	6 sc in magic ring. (6 sts)
R2	Inc in each st around. (12 sts)
R3	*Sc 1, inc* 6 times. (18 sts)
R4	*Sc 2, inc* 6 times. (24 sts)
R5	*Sc 3, inc* 6 times. (30 sts)
R6	*Sc 4, inc* 6 times. (36 sts)
R7	*Sc 5, inc* 6 times. (42 sts)
R8	*Sc 6, inc* 6 times. (48 sts)
R9	*Sc 7, inc* 6 times. (54 sts)
R10+11	Sc 54.
R12	*Sc 7, inv dec* 6 times. (48 sts)
R13+14	Sc 48.
R15	*Sc 6, inv dec* 6 times. (42 sts)
R16-19	Sc 42.

Begin adding fiberfill and continue adding as you close the piece.

R20	*Sc 5, inv dec* 6 times. (36 sts)
R21-23	Sc 36.
R24	*Sc 4, inv dec* 6 times. (30 sts)
R25	Sc 30.
R26	*Sc 3, inv dec* 6 times. (24 sts)
R27	Sc 24.
R28	*Sc 2, inv dec* 6 times. (18 sts)
R29	*Sc 1, inv dec* 6 times. (12 sts)
R30	Inv dec around 6 times. (6 sts)

Fasten off and leave a tail to close the piece. (photo 37)

Using straight pins, pin the head to the body between rounds 28-30. (photos 38+39) Rounds 17-22 of the head will be sewn onto the body. With the yarn needle, weave it into the head and then into the body. (photo 40) Continue all the way around. If needed, sew around the head twice to make sure it is secure and not floppy. Secure with a knot and hide inside the body. (photos 41+42)

FRONT LEGS: MAKE 2

Using tan yarn,

R1	6 sc in magic ring. (6 sts)
R2	Inc in each st around. (12 sts)
R3	*Sc 1, inc* 6 times. (18 sts)
R4	Sc 18.

Change to mustard yellow yarn,

R5-7	Sc 18.
R8	*Sc 1, inv dec* 6 times. (12 sts)
R9-17	Sc 12.

Add fiberfill to the leg, making sure to not overstuff.

R18	Sc 5. Do this by lining up the stitches on both sides of the leg, then inserting the hook into both stitches. Then sc as normal. (photos 43-46)

Fasten off and leave a tail for sewing. (photo 47)

Using straight pins, pin the legs to the front of the body near round 23. (photos 48+49) Place them right next to each other. With the yarn needle and the tail, sew the legs to the body. Weave the needle under both loops (the "V") from R18 of the legs and then into the body. (photos 50+51) Secure with a knot and hide inside the body. (photo 52)

BACK LEGS: MAKE 2

Using tan yarn,

R1	6 sc in magic ring. (6 sts)
R2	Inc in each st around. (12 sts)
R3	*Sc 1, inc* 6 times. (18 sts)
R4	Sc 18.

Change to mustard yellow yarn,

R5-9	Sc 18.
R10	*Sc 7, inv dec* 2 times. (16 sts)
R11-15	Sc 16.

Add fiberfill to the leg, making sure to not overstuff.

R16	Sc 7. Do this by lining up the stitches on both sides of the leg, then inserting the hook into both stitches. Then sc as normal. (photos 53-56)

Fasten off and leave a tail for sewing. (photo 57)

Using straight pins, pin the legs to the sides of the body between rounds 8-14. (photos 58-60) With the yarn needle and the tail, sew the legs to the body. Weave the needle under both loops (the "V") from R16 of the legs and then into the body. (photo 61) Secure with a knot and hide inside the body. (photos 62-64)

53 54 55 56

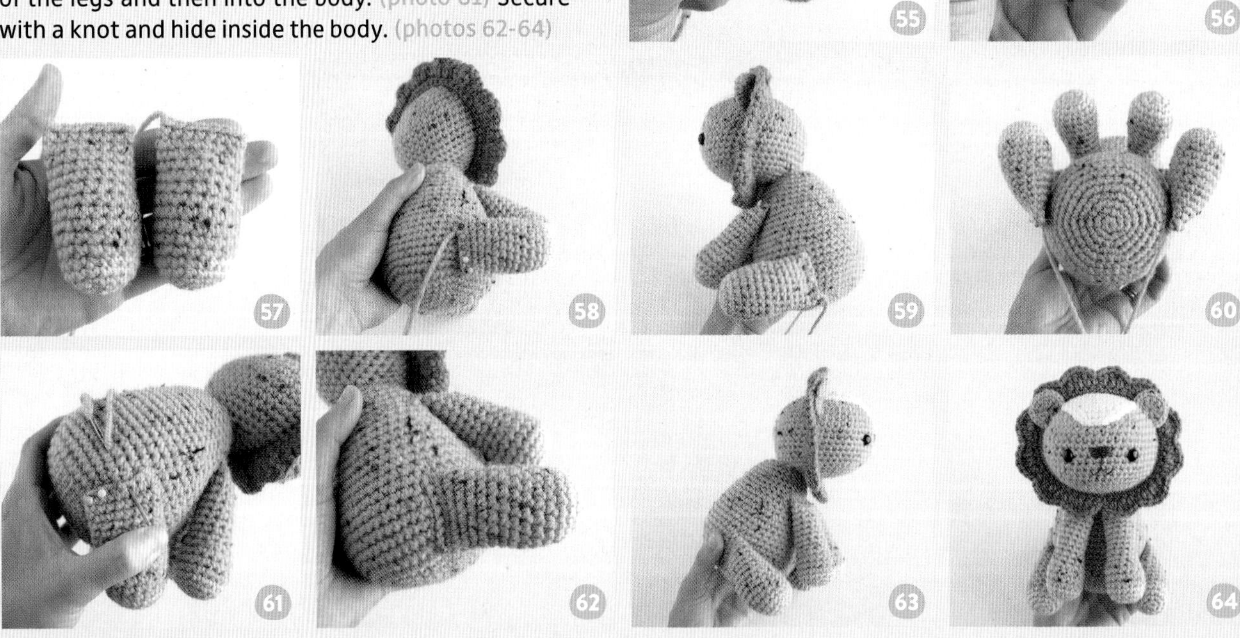

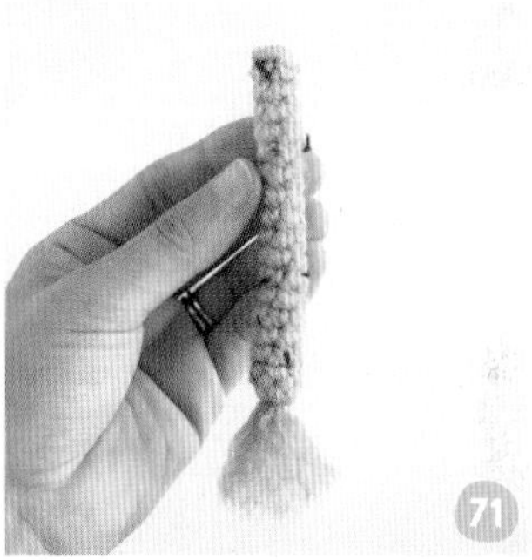

TAIL

Using mustard yellow yarn,

R1 6 sc in magic ring. (6 sts)

R2-18 Sc 6. After round 7 add the fur to the tail. (See below)

Fasten off and leave a tail for sewing. Leave the tail unstuffed.

To make the tail fur, cut 6 pieces, about 5 inches each of gold yarn. For each strand, tie a knot three times at one end. (photo 65) Then, using the yarn needle, weave through the opening of the tail and go through to the magic ring. (photo 66) Insert the needle into the center of the magic ring and pull the yarn through. Do this to each strand, one at a time. Once all six strands are woven through the magic ring, gently pull all strands and then trim to about an inch long. (photos 67+68) With the pet slicker brush, brush the strands so the yarn becomes fluffy. (photo 69) Use scissors, if needed, to shape the fur. (photo 70) Continue crocheting rounds 8-18. (photo 71)

Using straight pins, pin the tail to the body between rounds 9 and 10. (photo 72) With the yarn needle and the tail, sew into place. Sew the tail at a slight angle. Secure with a knot and hide inside the body. (photo 73)

73

ZEBRA

INTERMEDIATE

FINISHED MEASUREMENTS

- Approx. 4 inches wide by 9.5 inches tall by 7 inches long

MATERIALS

- Worsted weight yarn: Black and White
- Size F/3.75mm crochet hook
- One pair of 10mm safety eyes
- Polyester fiberfill stuffing
- Yarn needle
- Scissors
- Stitch marker
- Straight pins

ABBREVIATIONS

- BLO- Back Loops Only
- Ch- Chain
- Inc- Increase
- Inv Dec- Invisible Decrease
- R- Round/Row
- Sc- Single Crochet
- St/s- Stitch/es

Note: There are several color changes throughout this pattern. When changing colors, simply drop the old color, pick up the new color, and continue crocheting as normal. This pattern is written so that when there is a color change, all you have to do is carry the yarn up the couple of rounds where it was last dropped. Make sure to position the color changes on the pieces toward the back, like the ears and neck, or toward the center, like the legs and body.

HEAD

Using black yarn,

R1 6 sc in magic ring. (6 sts)
R2 Inc in each st around. (12 sts)
R3 *Sc 1, inc* 6 times. (18 sts)
R4 *Sc 2, inc* 6 times. (24 sts)
R5 *Sc 3, inc* 6 times. (30 sts)
R6 *Sc 4, inc* 6 times. (36 sts)
R7-9 Sc 36.

Change to white yarn,

R10+11 Sc 36.

Change to black yarn,

R12 Sc 36.

Change to white yarn,

R13+14 Sc 36.

Change to black yarn,

R15 Sc 36.

Change to white yarn,

R16 Sc 36.

Add the safety eyes between rounds 14 and 15, placing them 15 stitches apart.

R17 *Sc 5, inc* 6 times. (42 sts)

Change to black yarn,

R18 Sc 42.

Change to white yarn,

R19 *Sc 5, inv dec* 6 times. (36 sts)
R20 *Sc 4, inv dec* 6 times. (30 sts)

Begin adding fiberfill and continue adding as you close the piece.

Change to black yarn,

R21 *Sc 3, inv dec* 6 times. (24 sts)

Change to white yarn,

R22 *Sc 2, inv dec* 6 times. (18 sts)
R23 *Sc 1, inv dec* 6 times. (12 sts)

Change to black yarn,

R24 Inv dec around 6 times. (6 sts)

Fasten off and leave a tail to close the piece. (photos 1+2)

EARS: MAKE 2

Using white yarn,

R1 6 sc in magic ring. (6 sts)
R2 Sc 6.
R3 *Sc 1, inc* 3 times. (9 sts)

Change to black yarn,

R4 *Sc 2, inc* 3 times. (12 sts)

Change to white yarn,

R5 *Sc 3, inc* 3 times. (15 sts)
R6 *Sc 4, inc* 3 times. (18 sts)

Change to black yarn,

R7 Sc 18.

Change to white yarn,

R8+9 Sc 18.

Change to black yarn,

R10 *Sc 4, inv dec* 3 times. (15 sts)

Change to white yarn,

R11 *Sc 3, inv dec* 3 times. (12 sts)

Fasten off and leave a tail for sewing. Leave the ears unstuffed. (photo 3)

Pinch round 11 of the ears together. (photo 4) With the yarn needle and the tail, sew the pinched area together. (photos 5-7) This will give the ear a more pointed shape that looks natural. (photos 8+9) Using straight pins, pin the ears between rounds 18-20 on both sides of the head and about 13 stitches apart. (photos 10-12) The ears will line up 4 rounds behind the safety eyes. With the yarn needle and the tail, sew into place. Secure with a knot and hide inside the head. (photo 13)

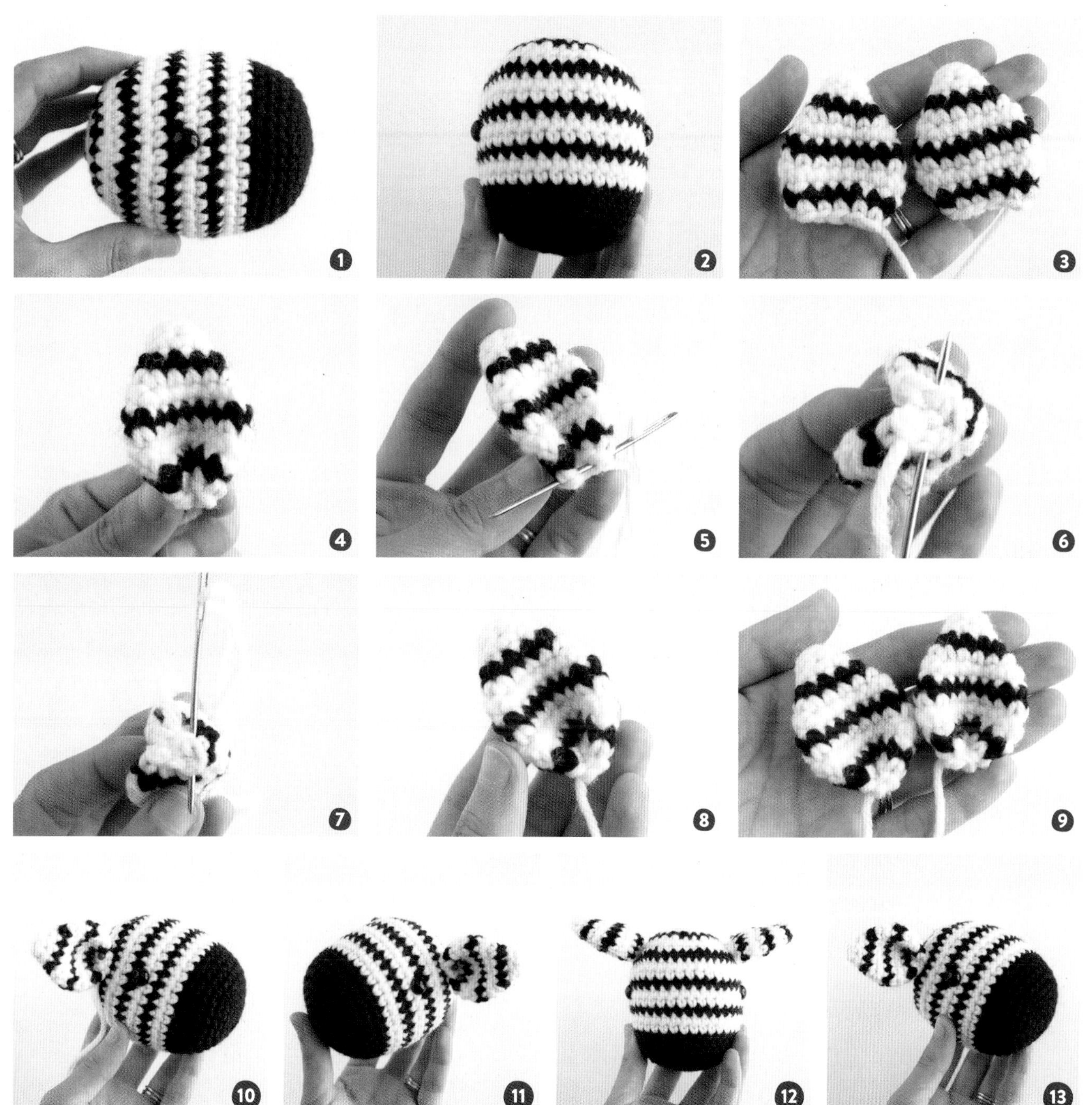
1
2
3
4
5
6
7
8
9
10
11
12
13

NECK

Using white yarn,

Leave about 12 inches at the beginning for sewing.

R1 Ch 18 then in the 1st ch, insert the hook into the top loop and make a sc. This will join the piece to form a circle. (photos 14-16) Place a stitch marker in this sc, as it will mark the END of the round. (photo 17) Then, in both loops, leaving the back "bump", sc around the chain. (18 sts) (photos 18+19) Pull the tail left at the beginning through the circle. (photos 20+21)

R2 Sc 18. (photo 22)

Change to black yarn,

R3 Sc 18.

Change to white yarn,

R4+5 Sc 18.

Change to black yarn,

R6 Sc 18.

Change to white yarn,

R7+8 Sc 18.

Fasten off and leave a tail for sewing. (photo 23)

Using straight pins, pin the neck between rounds 14-20 on the head, making sure to position the color change toward the back. (photos 24-26) Use the tail left at the end to sew the neck to the head. Weave the needle through the head and then under both loops (the "V") of the stitches from R8 of the neck. Secure with a knot and hide inside the head. The tail left at the beginning will be used to sew the neck to the body. Add fiberfill to the neck.

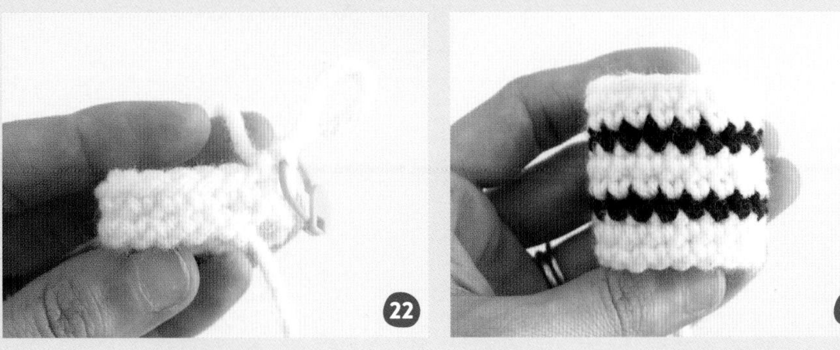

MANE

Using black yarn,

R1	Ch 16 then starting in the 2nd ch from the hook and in both loops, leaving the back "bump", sc in each chain across. (15 sts) Ch 1 and turn. (photos 27-29)
R2	Inc, sc 13, inc. (17 sts) Ch 1 and turn. (photo 30)
R3	Sc 17.

Fasten off and leave a long tail for sewing. (photo 31)

Using straight pins, pin the mane to the head, starting at round 16 and ending where the neck and head meet. (photos 32+33) Use the yarn needle to weave the long tail along the edge of the mane to get to row 1. Then sew the mane to the head. Weave the needle through the back "bumps" left over from R1 of the mane, then into the head. (photos 34+35) Continue doing this until you reach the end. Weave the starting tail into the head. Secure both tails with a knot and hide inside the head. (photos 36-39)

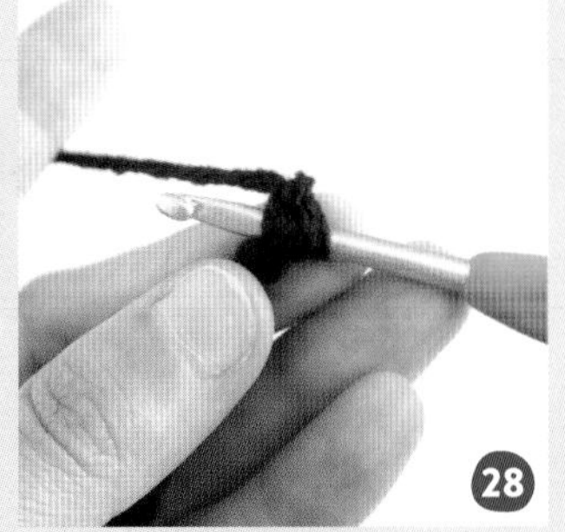

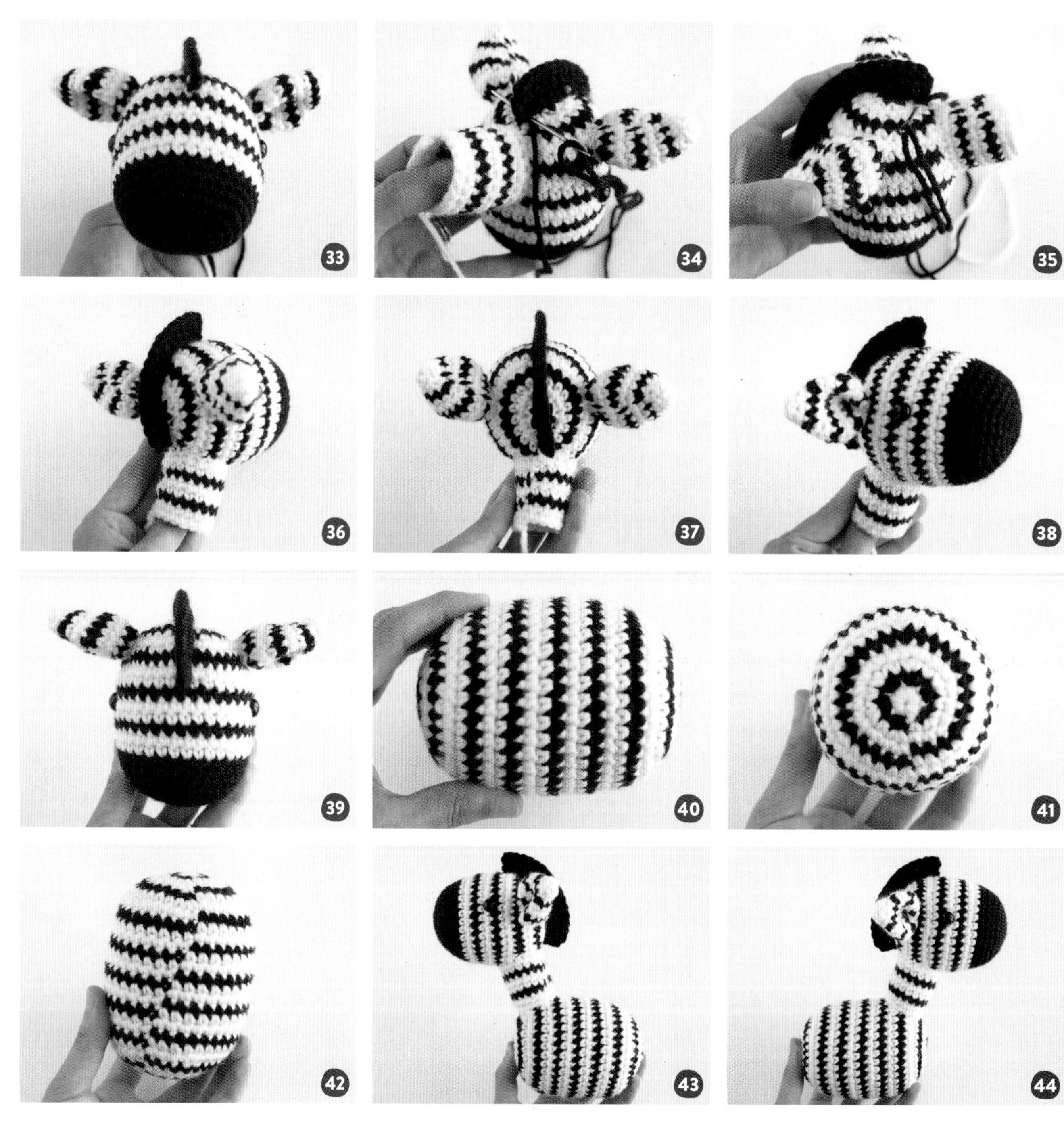
33
34
35
36
37
38
39
40
41
42
43
44

BODY

Using white yarn,

R1 6 sc in magic ring. (6 sts)

Change to black yarn,

R2 Inc in each st around. (12 sts)

Change to white yarn,

R3 *Sc 1, inc* 6 times. (18 sts)

R4 *Sc 2, inc* 6 times. (24 sts)

Change to black yarn,

R5 *Sc 3, inc* 6 times. (30 sts)

Change to white yarn,

R6 *Sc 4, inc* 6 times. (36 sts)

R7 Sc 36.

Change to black yarn,

R8 Sc 36.

Change to white yarn,

R9+10 Sc 36.

Change to black yarn,

R11 Sc 36.

Change to white yarn,

R12+13 Sc 36.

Change to black yarn,

R14 Sc 36.

Change to white yarn,

R15+16 Sc 36.

Change to black yarn,

R17 Sc 36.

Change to white yarn,

R18+19 Sc 36.

Change to black yarn,

R20 Sc 36.

Change to white yarn,

R21+22 Sc 36.

Change to black yarn,

R23 *Sc 4, inv dec* 6 times. (30 sts)

Change to white yarn,

R24 *Sc 3, inv dec* 6 times. (24 sts)

Begin adding fiberfill and continue adding as you close the piece.

R25 *Sc 2, inv dec* 6 times. (18 sts)

Change to black yarn,

R26 *Sc 1, inv dec* 6 times. (12 sts)

Change to white yarn,

R27 Inv dec around 6 times. (6 sts)

Fasten off and leave a tail to close the piece. (photos 40-42)

Using straight pins, pin the neck between rounds 6-11 on the body. Keep all the color changes on the underside of the body. Use the tail left at the beginning of the neck pattern to sew the neck to the body. Weave the needle through the back "bumps" left over from R1 of the neck, then into the body. Continue doing this until you reach the end. Add more fiberfill if needed before closing the piece. Secure with a knot and hide inside the body. (photos 43-45)

LEGS: MAKE 4

Using black yarn,

R1	7 sc in magic ring. (7 sts)
R2	Inc in each st around. (14 sts)
R3	In BLO, Sc 14.
R4	Sc 14.

Change to white yarn,

R5+6	Sc 14.

Change to black yarn,

R7	Sc 14.

Change to white yarn,

R8+9	Sc 14.

Change to black yarn,

R10	Sc 14.

Change to white yarn,

R11	Sc 14.

Fasten off and leave a tail for sewing. Add fiberfill to the legs. (photo 46)

Using straight pins, pin the legs to the body. Place the front legs between rounds 8-13 and use the yarn needle to sew into place. (photos 47-49) The front legs should be about 2 stitches apart from each other. Then place the back legs between rounds 18-23 and sew into place. (photos 50-52) The back legs should be about 1 stitch apart from each other. Secure with a knot and hide inside the body. (photo 53)

TAIL

Using white yarn,

R1	6 sc in magic ring. (6 sts)
R2	Sc 6.

Change to black yarn,

R3	Sc 6.

Change to white yarn,

R4	Sc 6.

Change to black yarn,

R5	Sc 6.

Change to white yarn,

R6 Sc 6.

Change to black yarn,

R7 Sc 6.

Change to white yarn,

R8 Sc 6.

Fasten off and leave a tail for sewing. Leave the tail unstuffed. (photo 54)

To make the tail tuft, cut 3 pieces, about 5 inches each of black yarn. For each strand, tie a knot three times at one end. Then, using the yarn needle, weave through the opening of the tail and go through to the magic ring. (photo 55) Insert the needle into the center of the magic ring and pull the yarn through. (photos 56+57) Do this to each strand, one at a time. Once all three strands are woven through the magic ring, cut the strands to the desired length, about an inch long. (photo 58) With the yarn needle, separate each strand so the hair becomes fluffy. (photos 59+60)

Using straight pins, pin the tail to the body near round 23. With the yarn needle and the tail, sew into place. Secure with a knot and hide inside the body. (photos 61+62)

ARCTIC

BELUGA WHALE

BEGINNER

FINISHED MEASUREMENTS

- Approx. 3.5 inches wide by 3.5 inches tall by 11 inches long

MATERIALS

- Worsted weight yarn: White
- Size F/3.75mm crochet hook
- One pair of 10.5mm safety eyes
- Polyester fiberfill stuffing
- Yarn needle
- Scissors
- Stitch marker
- Straight pins

ABBREVIATIONS

- Ch- Chain
- Inc- Increase
- Inv Dec- Invisible Decrease
- R- Round/Row
- Sc- Single Crochet
- St/s- Stitch/es

BODY

Using white yarn,

R1	6 sc in magic ring. (6 sts)
R2	Inc in each st around. (12 sts)
R3	*Sc 1, inc* 6 times. (18 sts)
R4	*Sc 2, inc* 6 times. (24 sts)
R5	*Sc 3, inc* 6 times. (30 sts)
R6	*Sc 4, inc* 6 times. (36 sts)
R7	*Sc 5, inc* 6 times. (42 sts)
R8	*Sc 6, inc* 6 times. (48 sts)
R9-17	Sc 48.

Add the safety eyes between rounds 12 and 13, placing them 29 stitches apart, counting across the top. (photo 1)

R18	*Sc 6, inv dec* 6 times. (42 sts)
R19+20	Sc 42.
R21	*Sc 6, inc* 6 times. (48 sts)
R22	*Sc 7, inc* 6 times. (54 sts)
R23-31	Sc 54.

Begin adding fiberfill and continue adding as you work the piece.

R32	*Sc 7, inv dec* 6 times. (48 sts)
R33	Sc 48.
R34	*Sc 6, inv dec* 6 times. (42 sts)
R35-37	Sc 42.
R38	*Sc 5, inv dec* 6 times. (36 sts)
R39-41	Sc 36.
R42	*Sc 4, inv dec* 6 times. (30 sts)
R43-45	Sc 30.
R46	*Sc 3, inv dec* 6 times. (24 sts)
R47-49	Sc 24.
R50	*Sc 2, inv dec* 6 times. (18 sts)
R51-53	Sc 18.
R54	*Sc 1, inv dec* 6 times. (12 sts)
R55-57	Sc 12.
R58	Inv dec around 6 times. (6 sts)

Fasten off and leave a tail to close the piece. (photo 2)

1

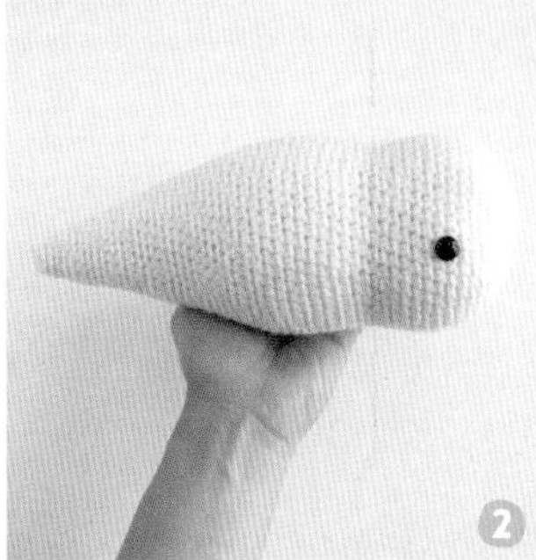
2

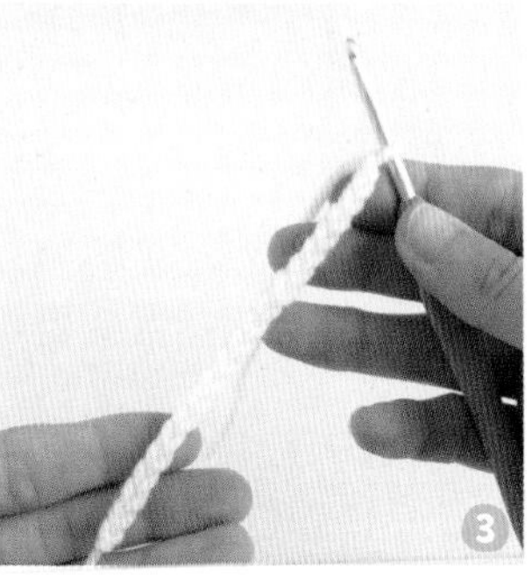
3

4

5

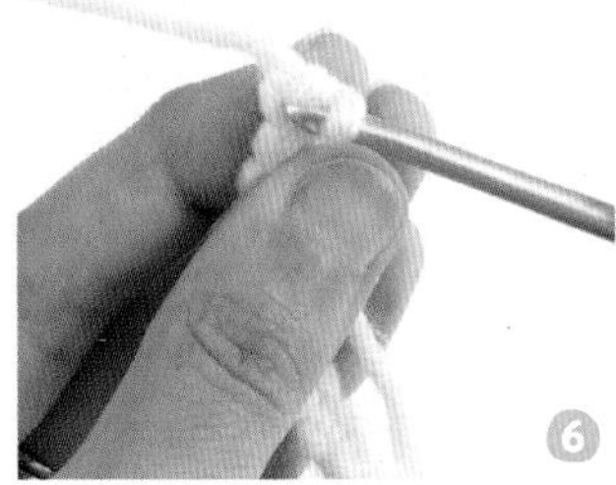
6

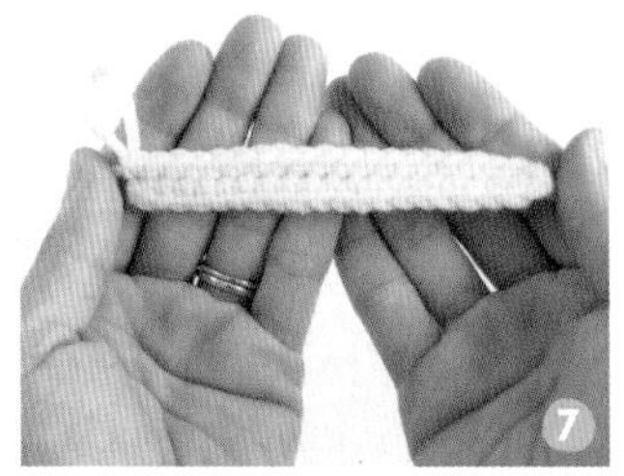
7

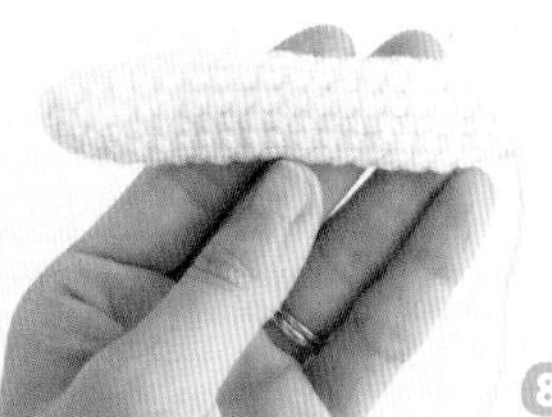
8

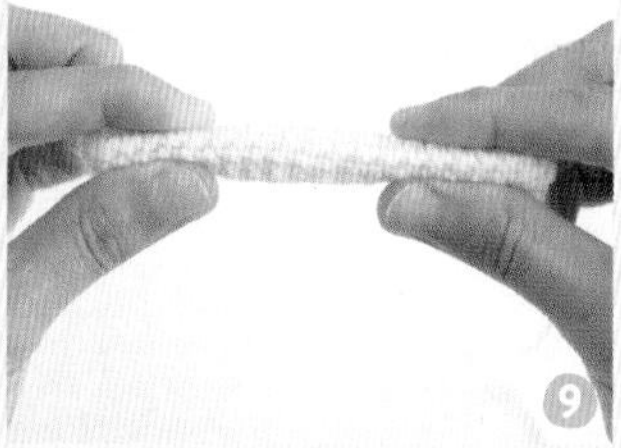

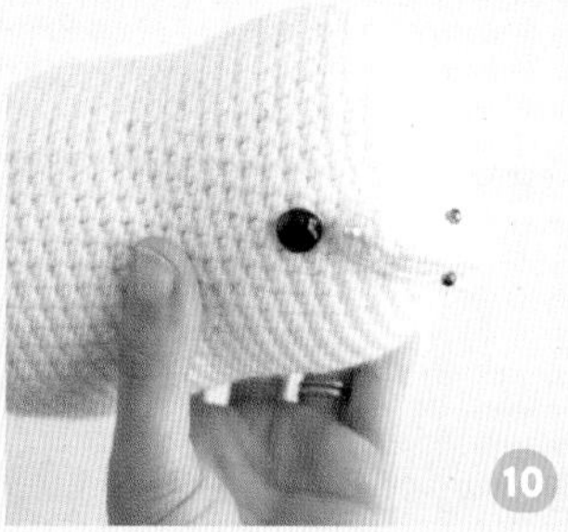

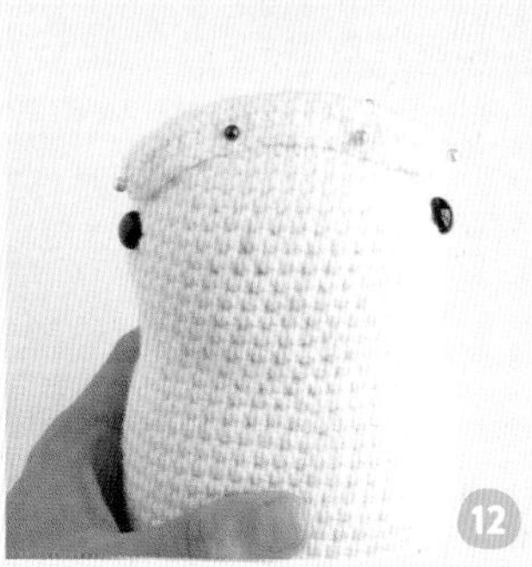

MOUTHPIECE

Using white yarn,

R1 Ch 21 then starting in the 2nd ch from the hook and in both loops, leaving the back "bump", sc in each chain across, 20 times. Then turn the work and sc across the back bumps 20 times. (40 sts) (photos 3-7)

R2 Sc 40.

Fasten off and leave a long tail for sewing. Leave the mouthpiece unstuffed. (photo 8)

Fold the mouth in half to create a nice center seam. (photo 9) Using straight pins, pin the mouth to the front of the body, starting from rounds 10 and 11 near one eye, then going to the other eye and pinning near rounds 10 and 11. (photos 10-12) The piece will span from one safety eye to the other and will be about 4 rounds down from the magic ring. (photo 13) Using the yarn needle and the tail, sew the mouth to the body. (photo 14) Secure with a knot and hide inside the body. (photos 15-18)

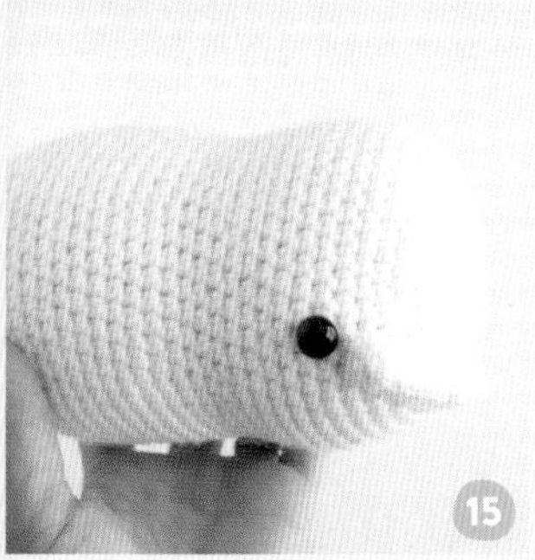

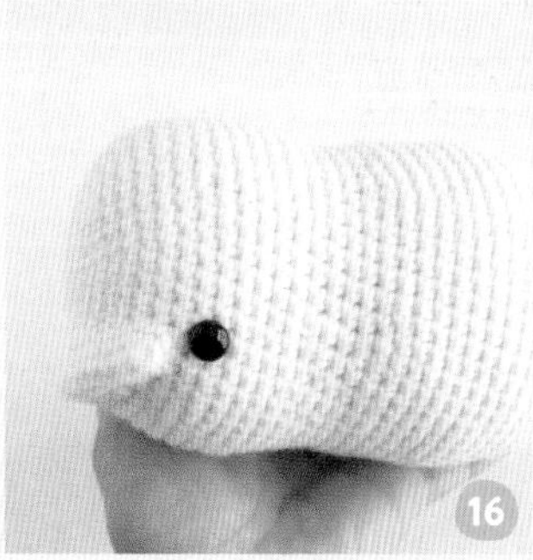

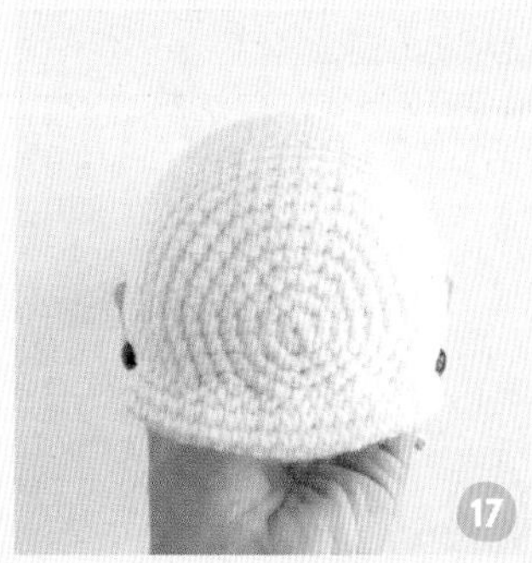

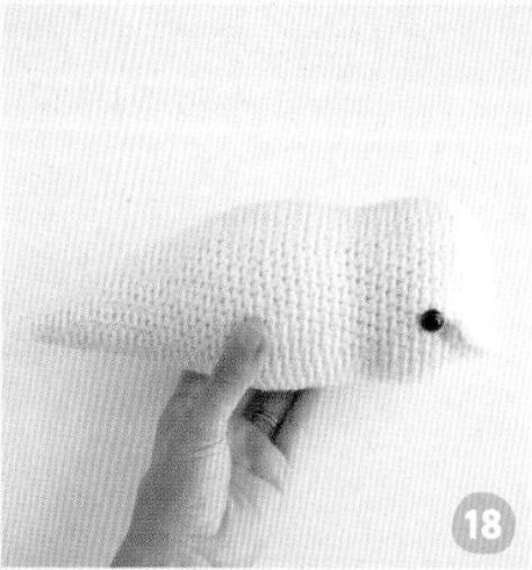

PECTORAL FINS: MAKE 2

Using white yarn,

R1	6 sc in magic ring. (6 sts)
R2	Inc in each st around. (12 sts)
R3	Sc 12.
R4	*Sc 1, inc* 6 times. (18 sts)
R5-8	Sc 18.
R9	*Sc 1, inv dec* 6 times. (12 sts)
R10	Sc 5. Do this by lining up the stitches on both sides of the fin, then inserting the hook into both stitches. Then sc as normal. (photos 19-22)

Fasten off and leave a tail for sewing. Leave the fins unstuffed. (photo 23)

Using straight pins, pin the fins to the sides of the body between rounds 23-27, pinning at a slight angle. (photos 24+25) With the yarn needle and the tail, sew the fins to the body. Weave the needle under both loops (the "V") from R10 of the fins and then into the body. (photo 26) Secure with a knot and hide inside the body. (photos 27-29)

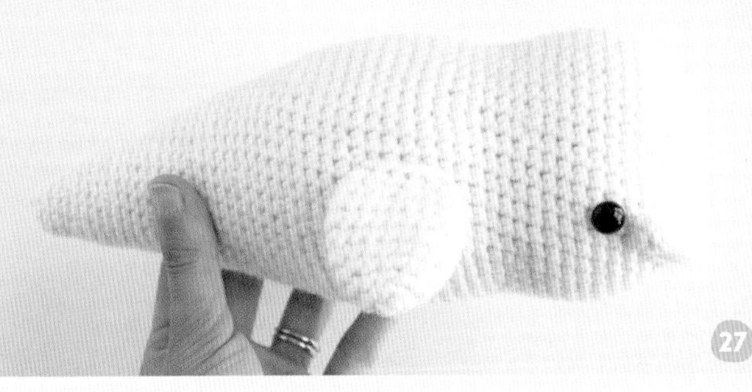

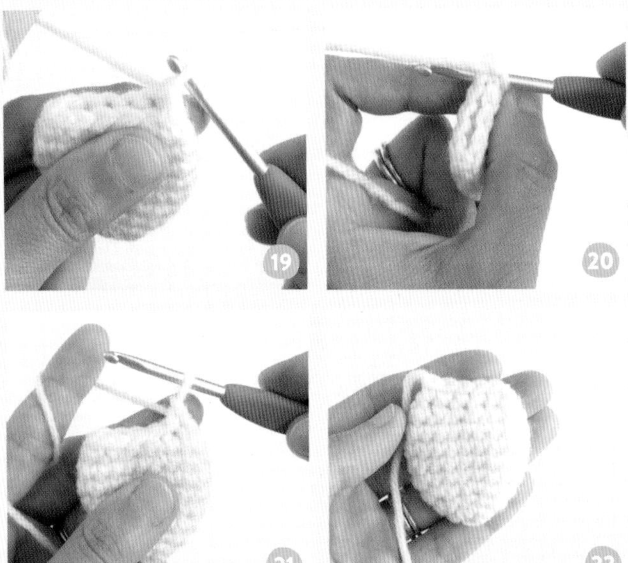

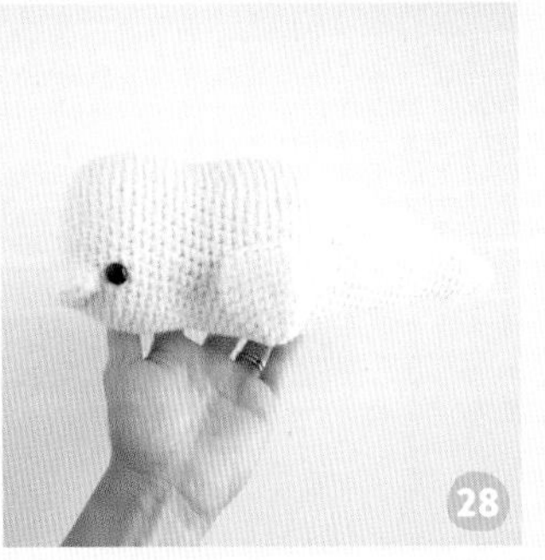

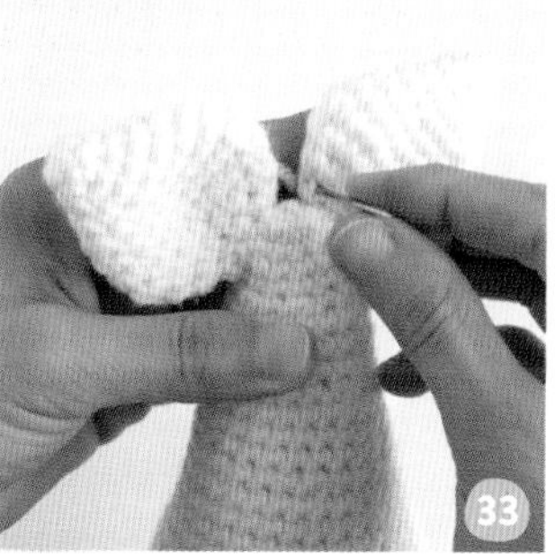

FLUKE: MAKE 2

Using white yarn,

R1	6 sc in magic ring. (6 sts)
R2	Sc 6.
R3	Inc in each st around. (12 sts)
R4	Sc 12.
R5	*Sc 1, inc* 6 times. (18 sts)
R6	Sc 18.
R7	*Sc 2, inc* 6 times. (24 sts)
R8	Sc 24.
R9	*Sc 2, inv dec* 6 times. (18 sts)
R10	*Sc 1, inv dec* 6 times. (12 sts)
R11	*Sc 2, inv dec* 3 times. (9 sts)

Fasten off and leave a tail for sewing. Leave each fluke unstuffed. (photo 30)

Using straight pins, pin each fluke to the side of the body between rounds 56-58. (photo 31) With the yarn needle and the tail, sew the flukes to the body. Secure only one yarn tail and hide inside the body. Leave the second yarn tail for this next step. With the yarn tail, sew the parts of the fins that are touching together. Only sew rounds 9-11 together. (photos 32-34) Secure with a knot and hide inside the body. (photos 35+36)

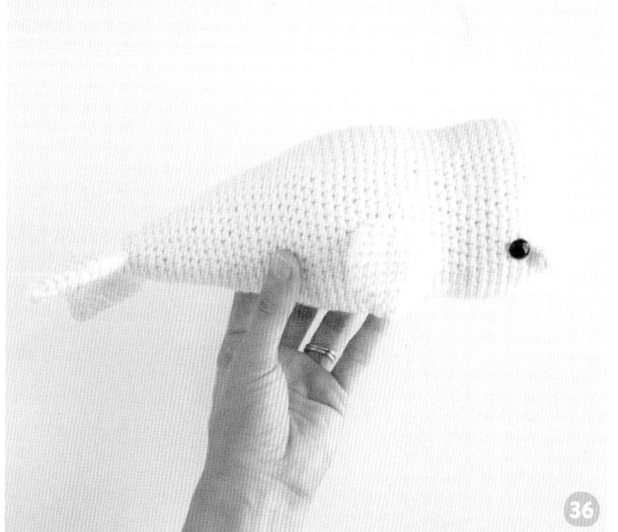

HARP SEAL PUP

BEGINNER

FINISHED MEASUREMENTS

- Approx. 4 inches wide by 4 inches tall by 9 inches long

MATERIALS

- Worsted weight yarn: Cream
- Size F/3.75mm crochet hook
- One pair of 10mm safety eyes
- Black embroidery floss and needle
- Black felt
- Polyester fiberfill stuffing
- Yarn needle
- Scissors
- Stitch marker
- Straight pins

ABBREVIATIONS

- Inc- Increase
- Inv Dec- Invisible Decrease
- R- Round/Row
- Sc- Single Crochet
- St/s- Stitch/es

BODY

Using cream yarn,

R1	6 sc in magic ring. (6 sts)
R2	Inc in each st around. (12 sts)
R3	*Sc 1, inc* 6 times. (18 sts)
R4	*Sc 2, inc* 6 times. (24 sts)
R5	*Sc 3, inc* 6 times. (30 sts)
R6	*Sc 4, inc* 6 times. (36 sts)
R7	*Sc 5, inc* 6 times. (42 sts)
R8	*Sc 6, inc* 6 times. (48 sts)

Add the safety eyes between rounds 5 and 6, placing them 13 stitches apart. (photo 1)

R9-12	Sc 48.
R13	*Sc 6, inv dec* 6 times. (42 sts)
R14+15	Sc 42.
R16	*Sc 5, inv dec* 6 times. (36 sts)
R17+18	Sc 36.
R19	*Sc 5, inc* 6 times. (42 sts)
R20	*Sc 6, inc* 6 times. (48 sts)
R21	*Sc 7, inc* 6 times. (54 sts)
R22-31	Sc 54.

Begin adding fiberfill and continue adding as you work the piece.

R32	*Sc 7, inv dec* 6 times. (48 sts)
R33	Sc 48.
R34	*Sc 6, inv dec* 6 times. (42 sts)
R35	Sc 42.
R36	*Sc 5, inv dec* 6 times. (36 sts)
R37	*Sc 4, inv dec* 6 times. (30 sts)
R38	*Sc 3, inv dec* 6 times. (24 sts)
R39	*Sc 2, inv dec* 6 times. (18 sts)
R40	*Sc 1, inv dec* 6 times. (12 sts)
R41	Inv dec around 6 times. (6 sts)

Fasten off and leave a tail to close the piece. (photo 2)

NOSE

Using cream yarn,

R1	6 sc in magic ring. (6 sts)
R2	Inc in each st around. (12 sts)
R3	Sc 1, inc in the next three sts, sc 3, inc in the next three sts, sc 2. (18 sts) (photo 3)
R4	Sc 18.

Fasten off and leave a tail for sewing. (photo 4)

With the black felt, cut out a small oval for the nose. (photo 5) With black embroidery floss and a needle, sew the black felt near round 2 of the nose. (photo 6) Using the same strand of floss, stitch the mouth right below the nose. Stitch one line vertically, starting at the bottom center of the nose and ending in the middle of round 2. Then make two horizontal lines across round 2 to finish the mouth. (photo 7) For the whiskers, take the black embroidery floss and separate it into 3 strands total. (photo 8) Tie a knot at one end and thread the other end onto the needle. Insert the needle from the inside of the nose near round 2 and pull through to the outside. (photo 9) Cut to about 1 inch. Make 3 whiskers on each side of the black nose. Finally, separate each whisker into 3 strands so it looks fuller. (photo 10)

Using straight pins, pin the nose to the body over rounds 1-4. The nose will go right between the safety eyes. (photo 11) With the yarn needle and the tail, sew the nose to the body. Add fiberfill to the nose before closing the piece. Secure with a knot and hide inside the body. (photos 12+13)

1
2
3
4
5
6
7
8
9
10
11
12
13

FRONT FLIPPERS: MAKE 2

Using cream yarn,

R1	6 sc in magic ring. (6 sts)
R2	Inc in each st around. (12 sts)
R3	*Sc 1, inc* 6 times. (18 sts)
R4	Sc 18.
R5	*Sc 7, inv dec* 2 times. (16 sts)

With black embroidery floss, create 5 claws over round 3, spacing them evenly apart. (photo 14)

R6	*Sc 6, inv dec* 2 times. (14 sts)
R7	*Sc 5, inv dec* 2 times. (12 sts)
R8+9	Sc 12.

Fasten off and leave a tail for sewing. Leave the flippers unstuffed. (photo 15)

Using straight pins, pin the flippers to the sides of the body between rounds 18-20. The flippers should be about 5 stitches apart. (photos 16+17) Make sure to pin the flippers at a slight angle. With the yarn needle and the tail, sew the flippers to the body. Secure with a knot and hide inside the body. (photos 18+19)

HIND FLIPPERS: MAKE 2

Using cream yarn,

R1	6 sc in magic ring. (6 sts)
R2	Inc in each st around. (12 sts)
R3	Sc 12.
R4	*Sc 1, inc* 6 times. (18 sts)
R5-9	Sc 18.
R10	*Sc 1, inv dec* 6 times. (12 sts)
R11	Sc 12.
R12	*Sc 1, inv dec* 4 times. (8 sts)

Fasten off and leave a tail for sewing. Leave the flippers unstuffed. (photo 20)

Using straight pins, pin the flippers to the end of the body between rounds 39-41. (photos 21+22) With the yarn needle and the tail, sew the flippers to the body. Secure with a knot and hide inside the body. (photos 23-25)

14

15

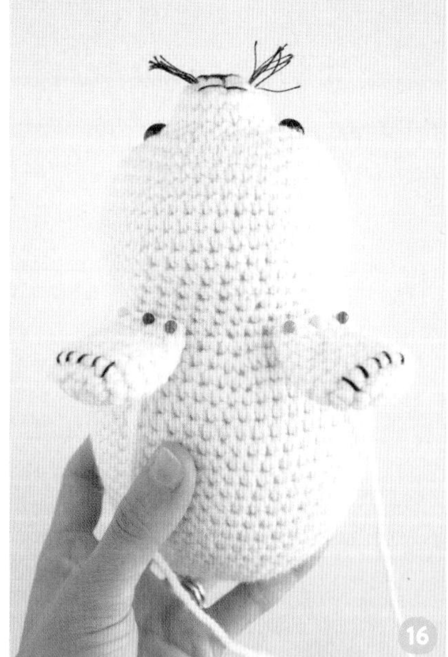
16

17
18
19
20
21
22
23
24
25

PENGUIN

INTERMEDIATE

FINISHED MEASUREMENTS

- Approx. 4.5 inches wide by 7 inches tall

MATERIALS

- Worsted weight yarn: White, Black, and Orange
- Size F/3.75mm crochet hook
- One pair of 10.5mm safety eyes
- Polyester fiberfill stuffing
- Yarn needle
- Scissors
- Stitch marker
- Straight pins

ABBREVIATIONS

- Ch- Chain
- Dec- Decrease
- Inc- Increase
- Inv Dec- Invisible Decrease
- R- Round/Row
- Sc- Single Crochet
- St/s- Stitch/es

Note: The penguin head has a lot of color changes. I found it best to cut the yarn after each color change and rejoin it when needed. Just make sure to secure all the ends if you do this method. Another option is to carry the yarn behind the work and pick it up when needed. I didn't like this method, as the yarn being carried was visible through the stitches. Remember to leave loose tension on the color not being used if you do this method.

HEAD

Using black yarn,

R1 6 sc in magic ring. (6 sts)
R2 Inc in each st around. (12 sts)
R3 *Sc 1, inc* 6 times. (18 sts)
R4 *Sc 2, inc* 6 times. (24 sts)
R5 *Sc 3, inc* 6 times. (30 sts)
R6 *Sc 4, inc* 6 times. (36 sts)
R7 *Sc 5, inc* 6 times. (42 sts)
R8 *Sc 6, inc* 6 times. (48 sts)
R9 Sc 48.
R10 With black sc 14, with white sc 6, with black sc 7, with white sc 6, with black sc 15. (48 sts) (photo 1)
R11 With black sc 13, with white sc 8, with black sc 5, with white sc 8, with black sc 14. (48 sts)
R12 With black sc 13, with white sc 9, with black sc 4, with white sc 9, with black sc 13. (48 sts)
R13 With black sc 12, with white sc 11, with black sc 3, with white sc 10, with black sc 12. (48 sts)
R14 With black sc 12, with white sc 25, with black sc 11. (48 sts) (photo 2)
R15+16 With black sc 12, with white sc 26, with black sc 10. (48 sts)

Add the safety eyes between rounds 14 and 15, placing them 8 stitches apart. You'll want the black tip from round 13 to be in the center of the eyes.

R17 With black sc 6, inv dec, sc 4, with white sc 2, inv dec, *sc 6, inv dec* 2 times, sc 6, with black inv dec, sc 6, inv dec. (42 sts)
R18 With black sc 5, inv dec, sc 4, with white sc 1, inv dec, *sc 5, inv dec* 3 times, with black sc 5, inv dec. (36 sts)
R19 With black sc 4, inv dec, sc 4, with white inv dec, *sc 4, inv dec* 3 times, with black sc 4, inv dec. (30 sts)

Begin adding fiberfill and continue adding as you close the piece.

R20 With black *sc 3, inv dec* 2 times, with white *sc 3, inv dec* 3 times, with black sc 3, inv dec. (24 sts)
R21 With black *sc 2, inv dec* 2 times, with white *sc 2, inv dec* 3 times, with black sc 2, inv dec. (18 sts)
R22 With black *sc 1, inv dec* 2 times, with white *sc 1, inv dec* 3 times, with black sc 1, inv dec. (12 sts)
R23 With black inv dec 2 times, with white inv dec 3 times, with black inv dec. (6 sts)

Fasten off and leave a tail to close the piece. (photos 3-5)

BEAK

Using orange yarn,

R1 6 sc in magic ring. (6 sts)
R2 Sc 6.
R3 *Sc 1, inc* 3 times. (9 sts)

Fasten off and leave a tail for sewing. Leave unstuffed. (photo 6)

Using straight pins, pin the beak to the head between rounds 13-15. Make sure to place it in the middle of the safety eyes. With the yarn needle and the tail, sew the beak to the head. Secure with a knot and hide inside the head. (photo 7)

BODY

Using black yarn,

R1	6 sc in magic ring. (6 sts)
R2	Inc in each st around. (12 sts)
R3	*Sc 1, inc* 6 times. (18 sts)
R4	*Sc 2, inc* 6 times. (24 sts)
R5	*Sc 3, inc* 6 times. (30 sts)
R6	*Sc 4, inc* 6 times. (36 sts)
R7	*Sc 5, inc* 6 times. (42 sts)
R8	*Sc 6, inc* 6 times. (48 sts)
R9	*Sc 7, inc* 6 times. (54 sts)
R10+11	Sc 54.
R12	*Sc 7, inv dec* 6 times. (48 sts)
R13-15	Sc 48.
R16	*Sc 6, inv dec* 6 times. (42 sts)
R17-19	Sc 42.
R20	*Sc 5, inv dec* 6 times. (36 sts)

Begin adding fiberfill and continue adding as you work the piece.

R21-23	Sc 36.
R24	*Sc 4, inv dec* 6 times. (30 sts)
R25+26	Sc 30.
R27	*Sc 3, inv dec* 6 times. (24 sts)

Fasten off and leave a long tail for sewing. (photo 8)

BELLY

Using white yarn,

R1	Ch 9 then starting in the 2nd ch from the hook and in both loops, leaving the back "bump", sc in each chain across. (8 sts) Ch 1 and turn. (photos 9-11)
R2	Inc, sc 6, inc. (10 sts) Ch 1 and turn.
R3	Inc, sc 8, inc. (12 sts) Ch 1 and turn.
R4	Inc, sc 10, inc. (14 sts) Ch 1 and turn.
R5	Inc, sc 12, inc. (16 sts) Ch 1 and turn.
R6	Sc 16. Ch 1 and turn.
R7	Dec, sc 12, dec. (14 sts) Ch 1 and turn.
R8	Sc 14. Ch 1 and turn.
R9	Dec, sc 10, dec. (12 sts) Ch 1 and turn.

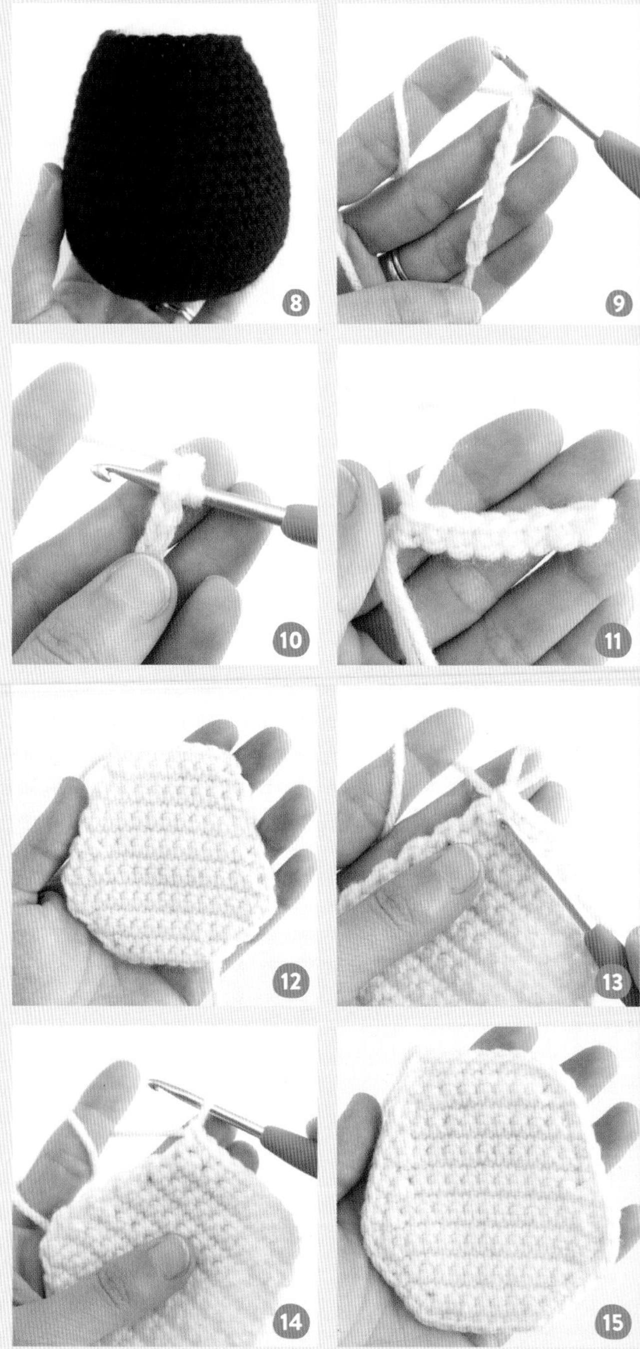

R10+11	Sc 12. Ch 1 and turn.
R12	Dec, sc 8, dec. (10 sts) Ch 1 and turn.
R13+14	Sc 10. Ch 1 and turn.
R15	Dec, sc 6, dec. (8 sts) Ch 1 and turn.
R16	Sc 8. (photo 12)

For this next row we are going to work around the edge of the belly.

R17	Sc in the same st as the last sc, then continue single crocheting all the way around the edge. Then sc 8 across the stitches from row 16. (48 sts) (photos 13-15)

Fasten off and leave an extra-long tail for sewing. Weave in the starting tail.

Using straight pins, pin the belly to the body between rounds 7-26. (photo 16) With the yarn needle and the tail, sew the belly to the body. Weave the needle under both loops (the "V") from the stitches on R17 of the belly and then into the body, coming out through one of the stitch holes. Insert the needle into the same stitch hole and then go over to the next stitch on the belly and repeat. (photos 17+18) Make sure to go under the stitches and not over them to create a clean finish. Secure with a knot and hide inside the body. (photo 19)

Using straight pins, pin the body to the head. (photos 20+21) With the yarn needle and the tail, sew the head in place on the body. If needed, add any extra fiberfill to the body before closing the piece. Secure with a knot and hide inside the body. (photo 22)

WINGS: MAKE 2

Using black yarn,

R1	6 sc in magic ring. (6 sts)
R2	Inc in each st around. (12 sts)
R3	Sc 12.
R4	*Sc 1, inc* 6 times. (18 sts)
R5-9	Sc 18.
R10	*Sc 1, inv dec* 6 times. (12 sts)
R11+12	Sc 12.
R13	Sc 5. Do this by lining up the stitches on both sides of the wing, then inserting the hook into both stitches. Then sc as normal. (photos 23-26)

Fasten off and leave a tail for sewing. Leave the wings unstuffed. (photo 27)

Using straight pins, pin the wings to the sides of the body between rounds 25-26. (photos 28-30) With the yarn needle and the tail, sew the wings to the body. Weave the needle under both loops (the "V") from R13 of the wings and then into the body. (photo 31) Secure with a knot and hide inside the body. (photo 32)

23

24

25

26

27

28

29

30

31

32

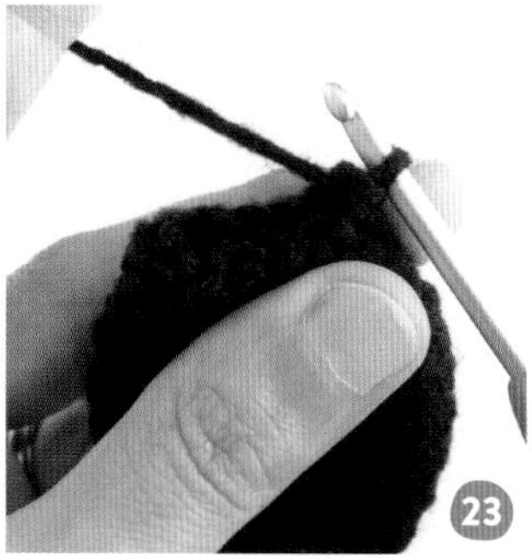

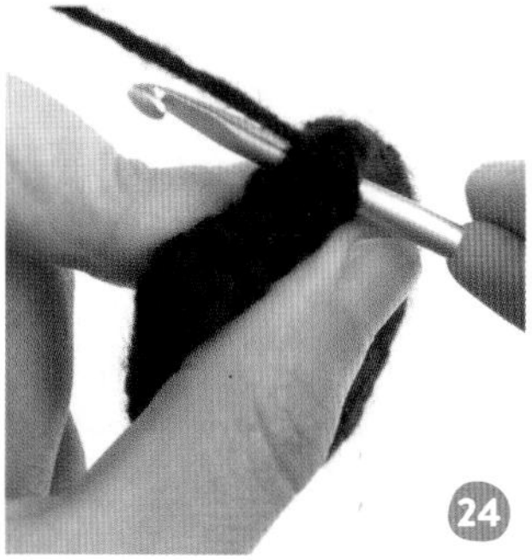

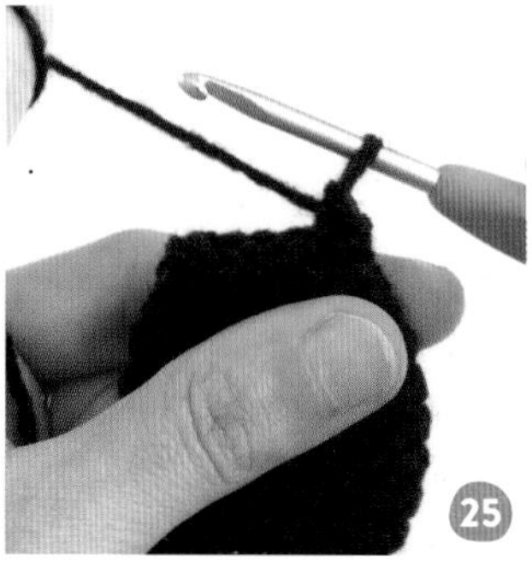

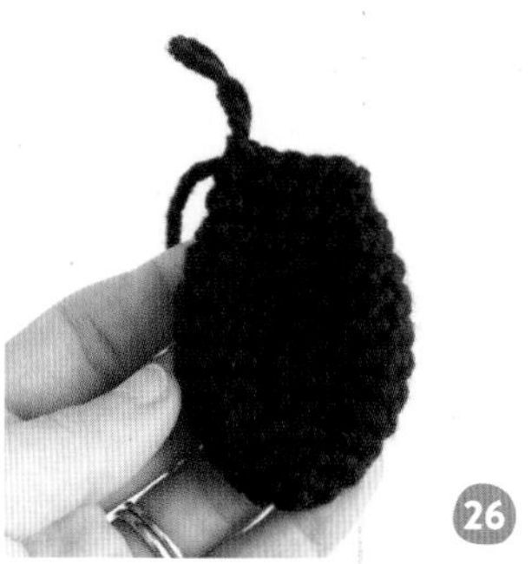

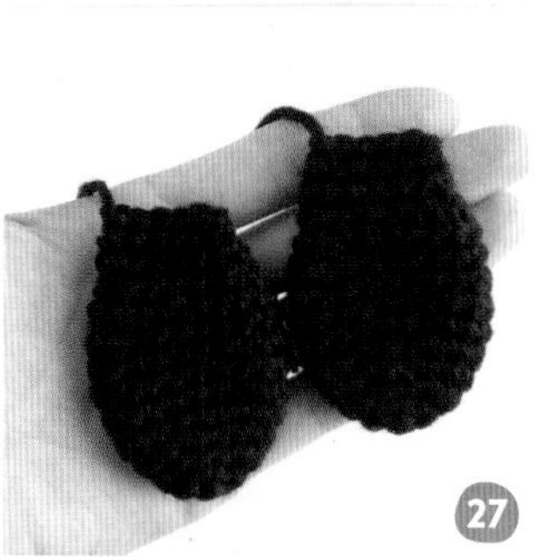

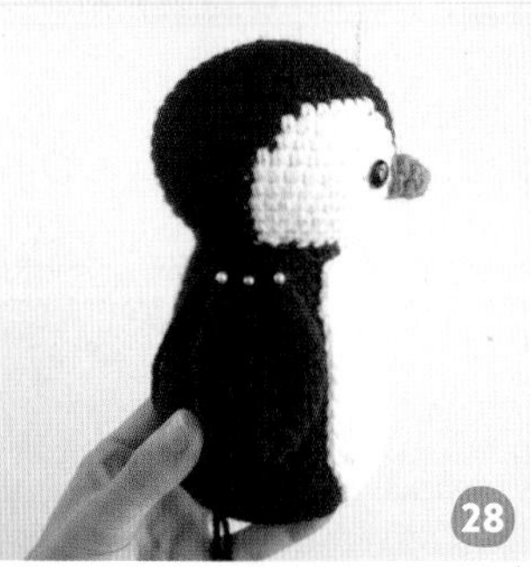

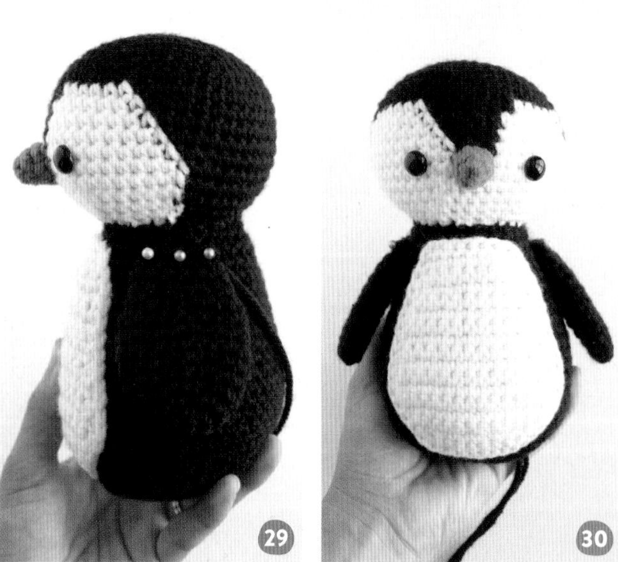

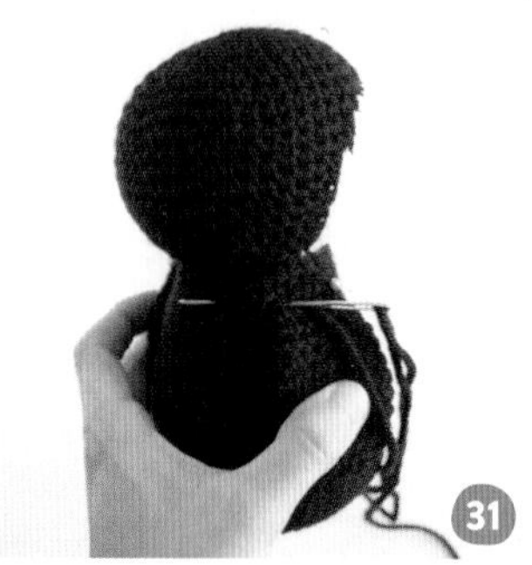

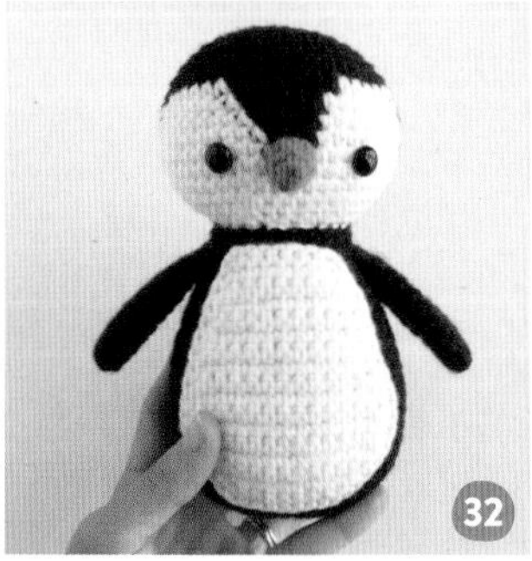

FEET: MAKE 2

Using orange yarn,

R1	Ch 7 then starting in the 2nd ch from the hook and in both loops, leaving the back "bump", sc in each chain across, 6 times. Then turn the work and sc across the back bumps, 6 times. (12 sts) (photos 33-37)
R2	Inc, sc 4, inc in the next two sts, sc 4, inc. (16 sts)
R3+4	Sc 16.
R5	*Inv dec, sc 6* 2 times. (14 sts)
R6	Sc 14.
R7	*Inv dec, sc 5* 2 times. (12 sts)
R8	Sc 12.
R9	Sc 5. Do this by lining up the stitches on both sides of the feet, then inserting the hook into both stitches. Then sc as normal. (photos 38+39)

Fasten off and leave a tail for sewing. Leave the feet unstuffed. (photo 40)

Using straight pins, pin the feet to the underside of the body between rounds 2-6. (photos 41+42) With the yarn needle and the tail, sew the feet to the body. Weave the needle under both loops (the "V") from R9 of the feet and then into the body. (photos 43+44)

With the same yarn tail, sew the outer part of the foot, rounds 6-9, to the body. (photos 45+46) Weave the needle through the foot, then into the body. (photo 47) Pull the needle through one of the stitch holes on the body, then insert into the same stitch hole and weave through to the foot. Repeat until you've sewn rounds 6-9 to the body. Then sew the top of the foot to the body; this will be round 7 on the foot. (photos 48+49) Once you reach the other side, sew the inner part of the foot to the body. Secure with a knot and hide inside the body. (photos 50+51)

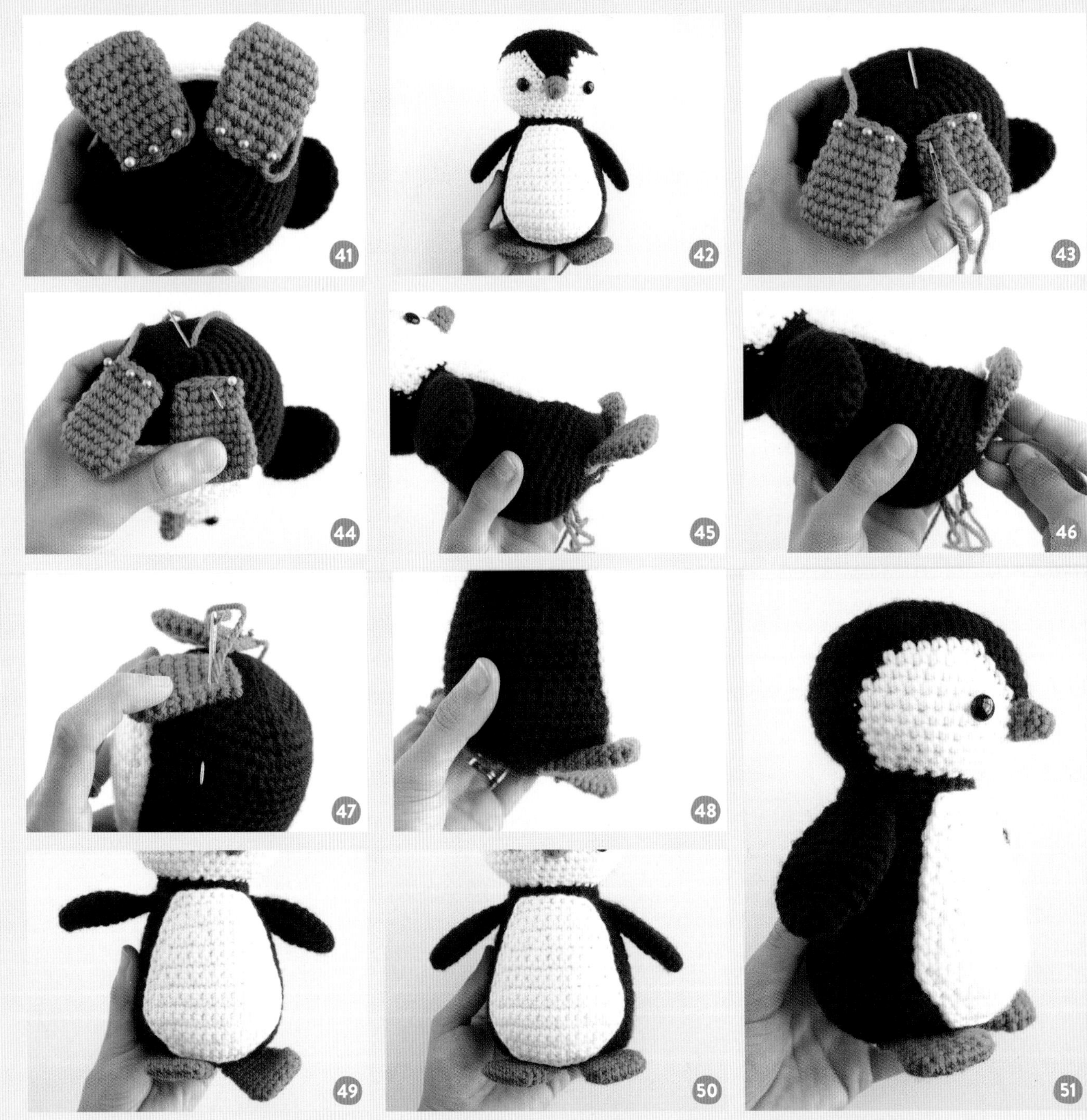
41
42
43
44
45
46
47
48
49
50
51

HAIR TUFTS: MAKE 3

Using black yarn,

R1 Ch 4 then starting in the 2nd ch from the hook, sc in each chain across. (3 sts)

Fasten off and leave a tail for sewing. (photo 52)

Using straight pins, pin the hair tufts to the head over rounds 1-2. (photo 53) With the yarn needle and the tail, sew the hairs in place. Secure each piece with a knot and hide the ends inside the head. (photos 54+55)

52

54

53

55

POLAR BEAR

BEGINNER

FINISHED MEASUREMENTS

- Approx. 6 inches wide by 10 inches tall when standing (7.5 inches tall when sitting)

MATERIALS

- Worsted weight yarn: White, Black, and Pink
- Size F/3.75mm crochet hook
- One pair of 10.5mm safety eyes
- Black embroidery floss and needle
- Black felt
- Polyester fiberfill stuffing
- Yarn needle
- Scissors
- Stitch marker
- Straight pins

ABBREVIATIONS

- Ch- Chain
- Inc- Increase
- Inv Dec- Invisible Decrease
- R- Round/Row
- Sc- Single Crochet
- St/s- Stitch/es

This friendly polar bear can easily be made in different colors. Try using brown yarn instead of white to create a cute brown bear!

HEAD

Using white yarn,

R1	6 sc in magic ring. (6 sts)
R2	Inc in each st around. (12 sts)
R3	*Sc 1, inc* 6 times. (18 sts)
R4	*Sc 2, inc* 6 times. (24 sts)
R5	*Sc 3, inc* 6 times. (30 sts)
R6	*Sc 4, inc* 6 times. (36 sts)
R7	*Sc 5, inc* 6 times. (42 sts)
R8	*Sc 6, inc* 6 times. (48 sts)
R9	*Sc 7, inc* 6 times. (54 sts)
R10-17	Sc 54.

Add the safety eyes between rounds 14 and 15, placing them 10 stitches apart.

R18	*Sc 7, inv dec* 6 times. (48 sts)
R19	*Sc 6, inv dec* 6 times. (42 sts)
R20	*Sc 5, inv dec* 6 times. (36 sts)

Begin adding fiberfill and continue adding as you close the piece.

R21	*Sc 4, inv dec* 6 times. (30 sts)
R22	*Sc 3, inv dec* 6 times. (24 sts)
R23	*Sc 2, inv dec* 6 times. (18 sts)
R24	*Sc 1, inv dec* 6 times. (12 sts)
R25	Inv dec around 6 times. (6 sts)

Fasten off and leave a tail to close the piece. (photo 1)

NOSE

Using white yarn,

R1	6 sc in magic ring. (6 sts)
R2	Inc in each st around. (12 sts)
R3	*Sc 1, inc* 6 times. (18 sts)
R4	*Sc 2, inc* 6 times. (24 sts)

Fasten off and leave a tail for sewing. (photo 2)

With black felt, cut out an oval nose. (photo 3) Using black embroidery floss, stitch the nose in place between rounds 2 and 4 using a running stitch. Next, stitch one line down, starting at the bottom center of the felt nose and ending near round 2 on the other side of the magic ring. (photo 4) Secure with a knot and trim the end.

Using straight pins, pin the nose to the head between rounds 12-19. The nose will go right between the safety eyes. (photos 5+6) With the yarn needle and the tail, sew the nose to the head. Weave the needle under both loops (the "V") from the stitches on R4 of the nose and then into the head, coming out through one of the stitch holes. Insert the needle into the same stitch hole and then go over to the next stitch on the nose and repeat. (photos 7+8) Make sure to go under the stitches and not over them to create a clean finish. Add fiberfill to the nose before closing the piece. Secure with a knot and hide inside the head. (photos 9+10)

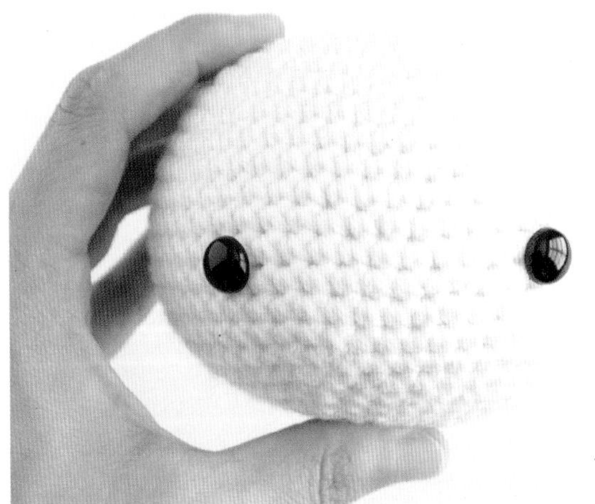

2
3
4
5
6
7
8
9
10

EARS: MAKE 2

Using white yarn,

R1	6 sc in magic ring. (6 sts)
R2	Inc in each st around. (12 sts)
R3	*Sc 1, inc* 6 times. (18 sts)
R4	*Sc 2, inc* 6 times. (24 sts)
R5	Sc 24.
R6	*Sc 2, inv dec* 6 times. (18 sts)
R7	*Sc 1, inv dec* 6 times. (12 sts)

Fasten off and leave a tail for sewing. Leave ears unstuffed. (photo 11)

Using straight pins, pin the ears to the head between rounds 7-12. (photos 12-14) With the yarn needle and the tail, sew the ears in place. Secure with a knot and hide inside the head. (photo 15)

INSIDE OF EARS: MAKE 2

Using pink yarn,

R1	4 sc in magic ring. (4 sts) Ch 1 and turn. (photos 16+17)
R2	Inc in each st around. (8 sts) (photos 18-20)

Fasten off and leave a tail for sewing. (photo 21)

Using straight pins, pin the inside pieces to the ears/head. (photo 22) With the yarn needle and the tail, sew each inside piece to an ear. Weave the needle under both loops (the "V") from R2 of the inside piece and then into the ear. Pull the needle through both layers of the main ear and come out the back side. Insert the needle into the same stitch hole, weaving through to the front side, and going over to the next stitch on the inside of the ear piece. This technique makes it so the stitching does not show on the back of the ear. (photos 23-26) Continue all the way around until you reach the end. Secure with a knot and hide inside the head. (photos 27+28)

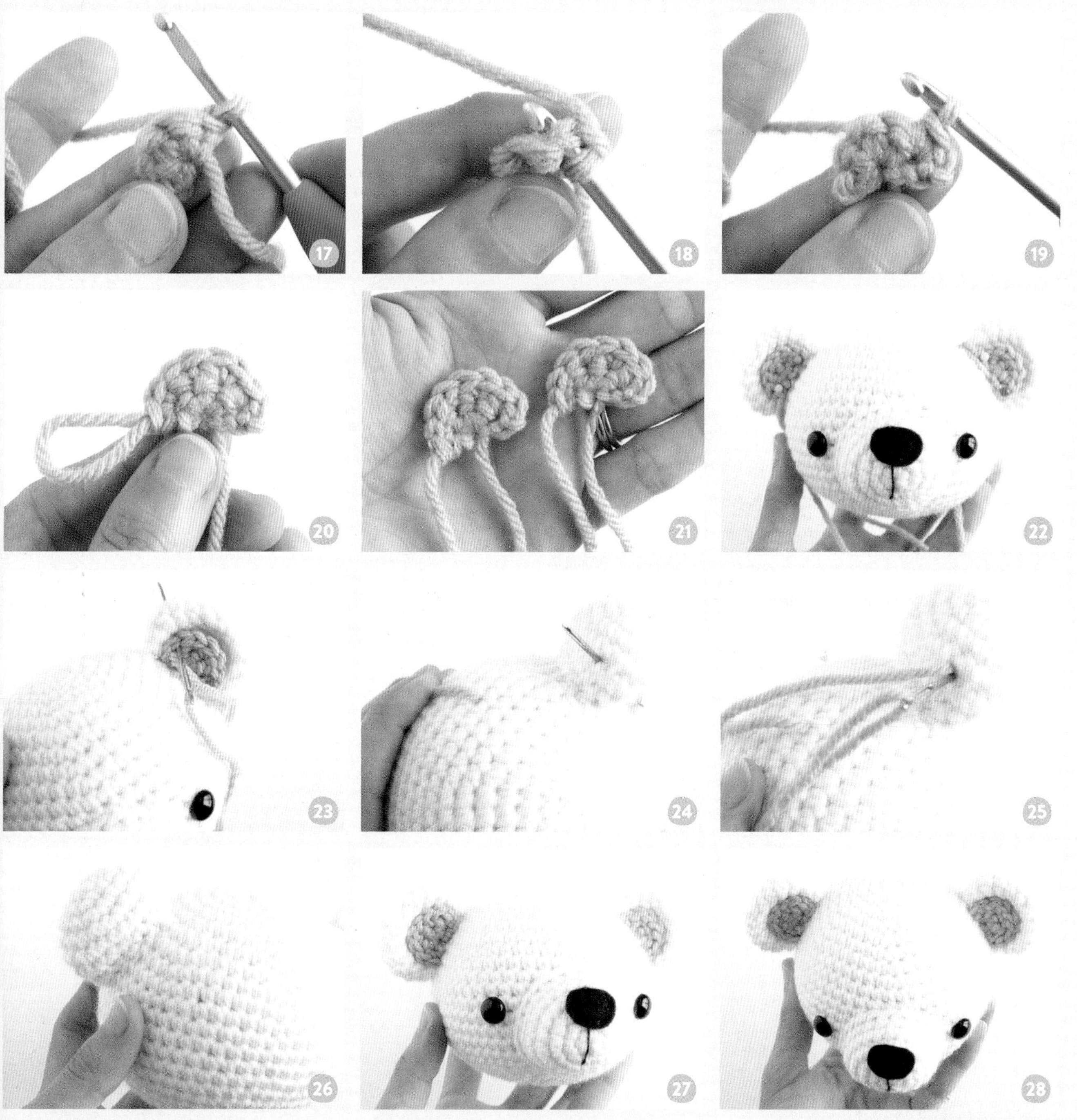
17
18
19
20
21
22
23
24
25
26
27
28

BODY

Using white yarn,

R1	6 sc in magic ring. (6 sts)
R2	Inc in each st around. (12 sts)
R3	*Sc 1, inc* 6 times. (18 sts)
R4	*Sc 2, inc* 6 times. (24 sts)
R5	*Sc 3, inc* 6 times. (30 sts)
R6	*Sc 4, inc* 6 times. (36 sts)
R7	*Sc 5, inc* 6 times. (42 sts)
R8	*Sc 6, inc* 6 times. (48 sts)
R9	*Sc 7, inc* 6 times. (54 sts)
R10-12	Sc 54.
R13	*Sc 7, inv dec* 6 times. (48 sts)
R14+15	Sc 48.
R16	*Sc 6, inv dec* 6 times. (42 sts)
R17-19	Sc 42.
R20	*Sc 5, inv dec* 6 times. (36 sts)

Begin adding fiberfill and continue adding as you work the piece.

R21-23	Sc 36.
R24	*Sc 4, inv dec* 6 times. (30 sts)
R25+26	Sc 30.
R27	*Sc 3, inv dec* 6 times. (24 sts)

Fasten off and leave a long tail for sewing. (photo 29)

Using straight pins, pin the body to the head. (photos 30+31) With the yarn needle and the tail, sew the head in place on the body. If needed, add any extra fiberfill to the body before closing the piece. Secure with a knot and hide inside the body. (photo 32)

PAW PADS: MAKE 2

Using black yarn,

R1	5 sc in magic ring. (5 sts)
R2	Inc in each st around. (10 sts)

Fasten off and leave a long tail for sewing. Set aside. (photo 33)

ARMS: MAKE 2

Using white yarn,

R1	6 sc in magic ring. (6 sts)
R2	Inc in each st around. (12 sts)
R3	*Sc 1, inc* 6 times. (18 sts)
R4-8	Sc 18.
R9	*Sc 4, inv dec* 3 times. (15 sts)

Begin adding fiberfill and continue adding as you work the piece.

R10-17	Sc 15.
R18	Sc 6. Do this by lining up the stitches on both sides of the arm, then inserting the hook into both stitches. Then sc as normal. (photos 34-37)

Fasten off and leave a tail for sewing.

Add the paw pad to the arm, placing it between rounds 4-8. (photo 38) With the yarn needle and the tail, sew the paw pad to the arm. Weave the needle under both loops (the "V") from R2 of the paw pad and then into the arm, coming out through one the the stitch holes. Insert the needle into the same stitch hole and then go over to the next stitch on the pad and repeat. (photos 39+40) Make sure to go under the stitches and not over them to create a clean finish. Leave the tail for making the toe pads.

With the leftover black yarn tail, make 5 evenly spaced toe pads around the top part of the paw pad. (photo 41) Go over each spot 3 times to build up a little bump. Secure with a knot and hide inside the arm. (photo 42)

Using straight pins, pin the arms to the sides of the body between rounds 16-22. (photos 43-45) Make sure to pin the arms at a slight angle. With the yarn needle and the tail, sew the arms to the body. Weave the needle under both loops (the "V") from R18 of the arms and then into the body. Secure with a knot and hide inside the body. (photos 46-48)

41
42
43
44
45
46
47
48

LEGS: MAKE 2

Using black yarn,

R1	6 sc in magic ring. (6 sts)
R2	Inc in each st around. (12 sts) Fasten off the black and leave a long tail for the toe pads.

Change to white yarn,

R3	*Sc 1, inc* 6 times. (18 sts) (photos 49-51)
R4	*Sc 2, inc* 6 times. (24 sts)
R5+6	Sc 24.
R7	Sc 6, inv dec 6 times, sc 6. (18 sts)
R8	Sc 6, inv dec 3 times, sc 6. (15 sts) (photo 52)

With the yarn needle and the black yarn tail, make 5 toe pads, stitching over round 4. (photo 53) You'll want the toe pads to be under the decreases from rounds 7 and 8. (photo 54) Go over each spot 4 times to build up a little bump. Each pad should be about one stitch apart. (photos 55+56) Secure with a knot and hide inside the leg.

Begin adding fiberfill and continue adding as you work the piece.

R9-18	Sc 15.
R19	Sc 6. Do this by lining up the stitches on both sides of the leg, then inserting the hook into both stitches. Then sc as normal. (photos 57-60)

Fasten off and leave a tail for sewing. (photos 61+62)

Using straight pins, pin the legs to the underside of the body between rounds 2-7. (photos 63+64) With the yarn needle and the tail, sew the legs to the body. Weave the needle under both loops (the "V") from R19 of the legs and then into the body. (photos 65+66) Secure with a knot and hide inside the body. (photos 67+68)

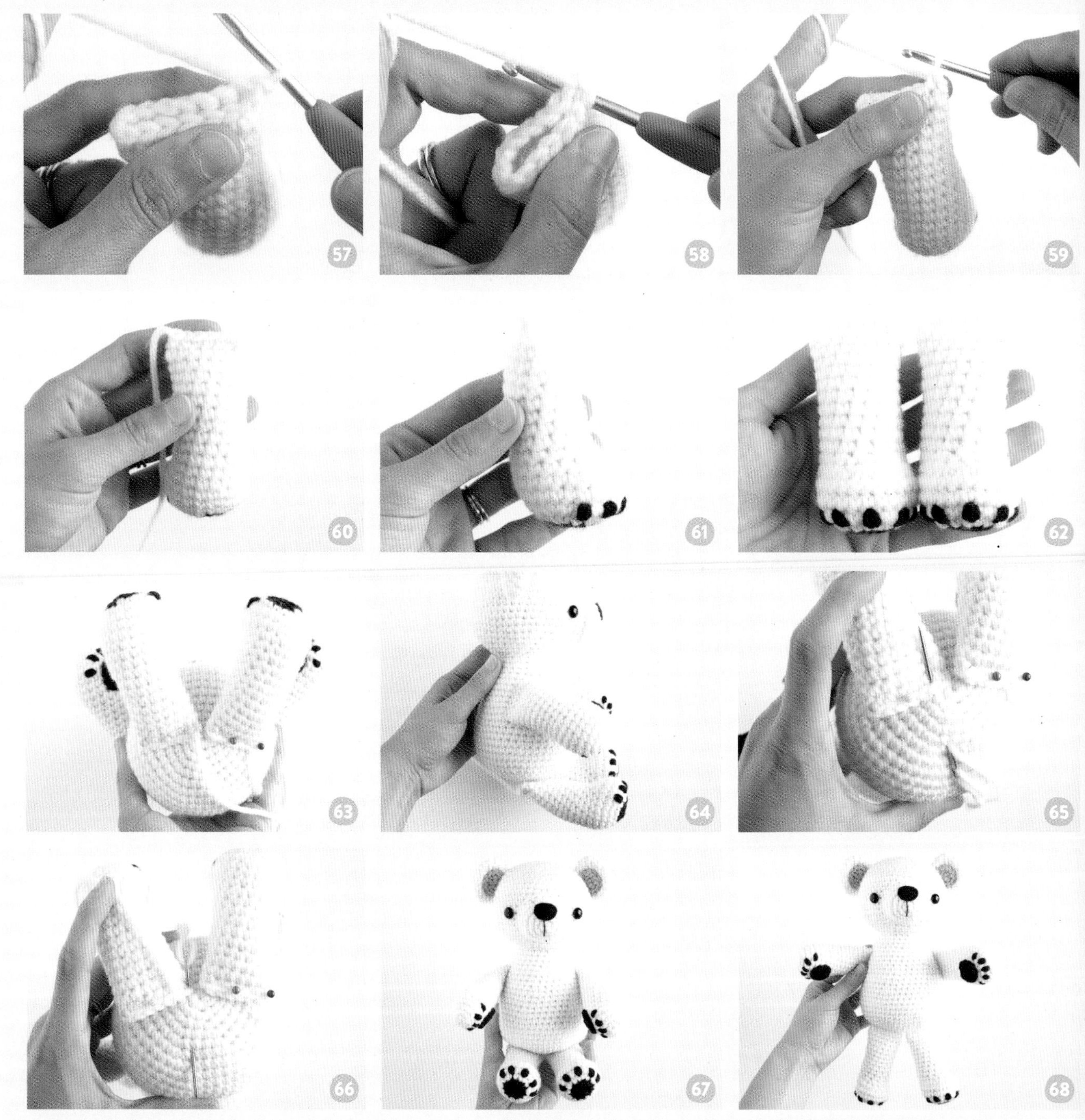
57
58
59
60
61
62
63
64
65
66
67
68

TAIL

Using white yarn,

R1	6 sc in magic ring. (6 sts)
R2	Inc in each st around. (12 sts)
R3	*Sc 1, inc* 6 times. (18 sts)
R4+5	Sc 18.

Fasten off and leave a tail for sewing. (photo 69)

Using straight pins, pin the tail to the body between rounds 8-13. (photo 70) With the yarn needle and the tail, sew the tail to the body. Make sure to add fiberfill to the tail before closing the piece. Secure with a knot and hide inside the body. (photos 71+72)

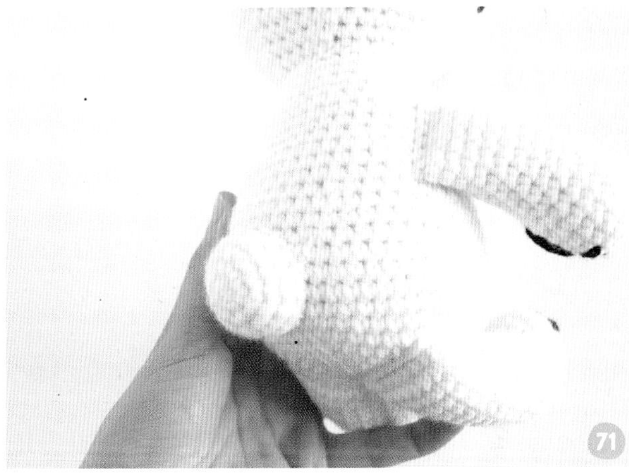

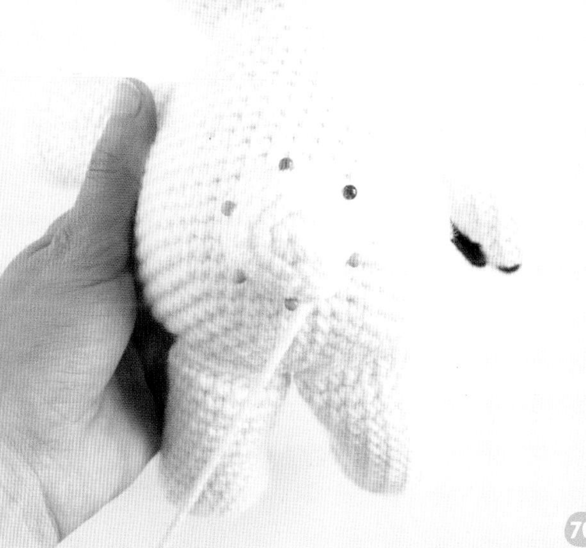

WALRUS

EXPERT

FINISHED MEASUREMENTS

- Approx. 5 inches wide by 5.5 inches tall by 9 inches long

MATERIALS

- Worsted weight yarn: Brown, Light Brown, and White
- Size F/3.75mm crochet hook
- One pair of 12mm safety eyes
- White embroidery floss and needle
- Brown felt
- Polyester fiberfill stuffing
- Yarn needle
- Scissors
- Stitch marker
- Straight pins
- Hot glue gun

ABBREVIATIONS

- Ch- Chain
- FLO- Front Loops Only
- Inc- Increase
- Inv Dec- Invisible Decrease
- R- Round/Row
- Sc- Single Crochet
- St/s- Stitch/es

BODY

Using brown yarn,

R1 6 sc in magic ring. (6 sts)
R2 Inc in each st around. (12 sts)
R3 *Sc 1, inc* 6 times. (18 sts)
R4 *Sc 2, inc* 6 times. (24 sts)
R5 *Sc 3, inc* 6 times. (30 sts)
R6 *Sc 4, inc* 6 times. (36 sts)
R7 *Sc 5, inc* 6 times. (42 sts)
R8 *Sc 6, inc* 6 times. (48 sts)
R9-13 Sc 48.
R14 *Sc 11, inc* 4 times. (52 sts)
R15 Sc 52.

Add the safety eyes between rounds 12 and 13, placing them 11 stitches apart.

R16 *Sc 12, inc* 4 times. (56 sts)
R17 Sc 56.
R18 *Sc 13, inc* 4 times. (60 sts)
R19 Sc 60.
R20 *Sc 9, inc* 6 times. (66 sts)
R21 Sc 66.
R22 *Sc 10, inc* 6 times. (72 sts)
R23-29 Sc 72.
R30 *Sc 10, inv dec* 6 times. (66 sts)
R31 Sc 66.
R32 *Sc 9, inv dec* 6 times. (60 sts)
R33 *Sc 8, inv dec* 6 times. (54 sts)
R34 *Sc 7, inv dec* 6 times. (48 sts)
R35 *Sc 6, inv dec* 6 times. (42 sts)
R36 *Sc 5, inv dec* 6 times. (36 sts)

Begin adding fiberfill and continue adding as you close the piece.

R37 *Sc 4, inv dec* 6 times. (30 sts)
R38 *Sc 3, inv dec* 6 times. (24 sts)
R39 *Sc 2, inv dec* 6 times. (18 sts)
R40 *Sc 1, inv dec* 6 times. (12 sts)
R41 Inv dec in each st around. (6 sts)

Fasten off and leave a tail to close the piece. (photo 1)

NOSE

The nose is worked in two pieces. First, crochet one side and then join where indicated in the pattern for the second side.

Using light brown yarn,

R1	5 sc in magic ring. (5 sts)
R2	Inc in each st around. (10 sts)
R3	*Sc 1, inc* 5 times. (15 sts)
R4	Sc 15.

Fasten off and leave a tail for sewing. Set aside. (photo 2)

Repeat rounds 1-4 to make a second side. Do not fasten off after round 4 and instead, follow the rounds listed below. We're going to connect the pieces and continue working on the nose.

R5 With the second nose piece still on the hook, insert the hook into the first stitch on the first nose piece and sc. (photos 3+4) This will be the stitch to the left of where we fastened off. Sc 15 times total on the first piece. Then on the second piece, you'll insert the hook into the first stitch we made in R4 for the second piece. Sc 15 times total on the second piece. (30 sts) (photos 5+6)

Use the yarn needle and the tail left over from the first nose piece to sew the opening between both pieces closed. (photos 7-9)

R6 Sc 30.

Fasten off and leave a long tail for sewing. Add fiberfill to each side of the nose. (photo 10)

For the whiskers, take the white embroidery floss and separate it into 3 strands total. (photo 11) Tie a knot at one end and thread the other end onto the needle. Insert the needle from the inside of the nose near rounds 2 and 3 and pull through to the outside. Cut to about 1.5 inches. (photo 12) Make 5 whiskers on each side of the nose. (photo 13) Finally separate each whisker into 3 strands so it looks fuller.

Using straight pins, pin the nose to the body between rounds 12-18. (photos 14+15) There should be one stitch between the nose and the safety eye on each side. With the yarn needle and the tail, sew the nose to the body. Make sure to add any extra fiberfill to the nose before closing the piece. Secure with a knot and hide inside the body. (photo 16)

Cut a small oval out of the brown felt. (photo 17) Use the hot glue gun to secure the felt to the center of the nose, where the nose and body meet. (photo 18)

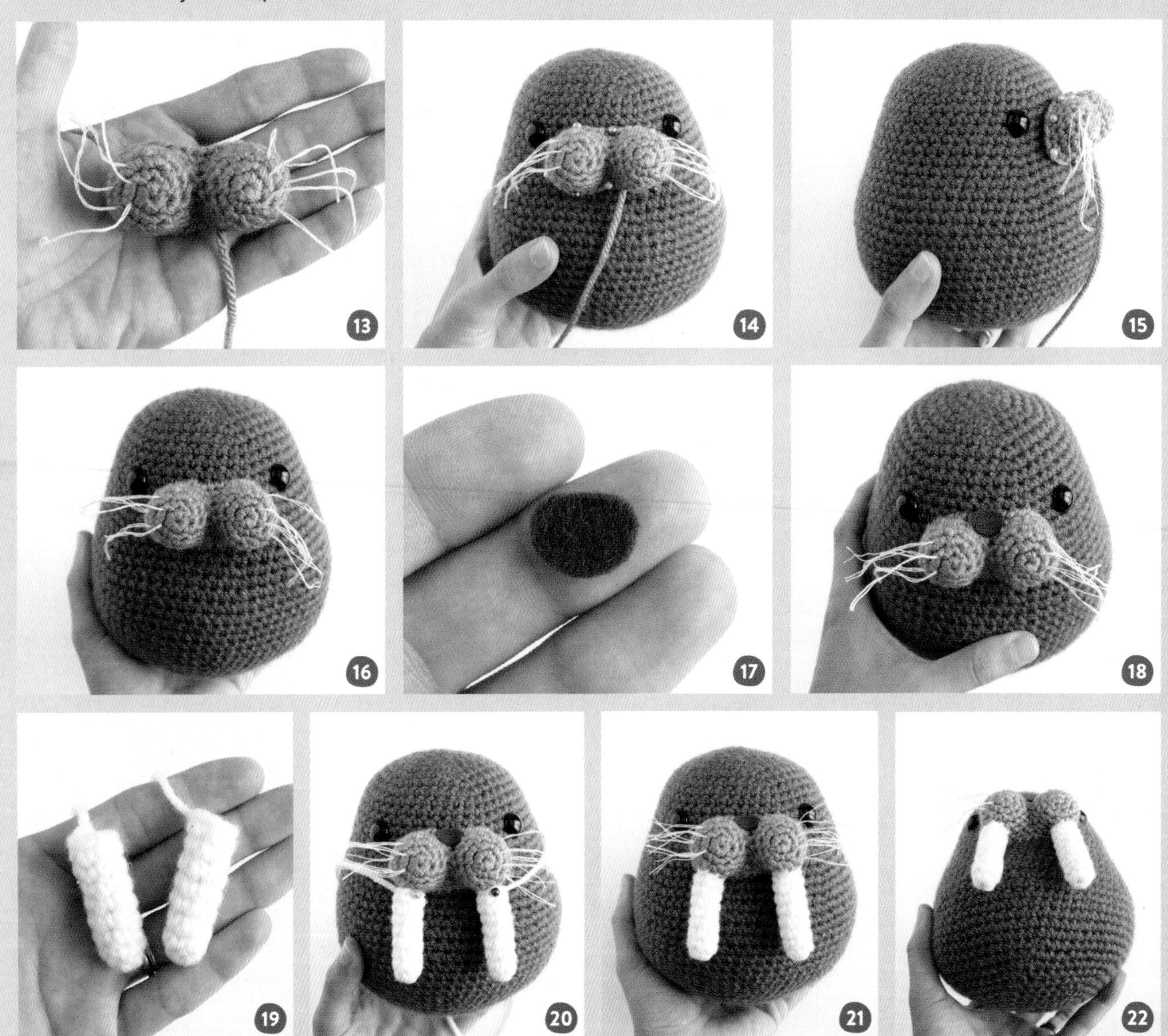

TUSKS: MAKE 2

Using white yarn,

R1	7 sc in magic ring. (7 sts)
R2-8	Sc 7.

Fasten off and leave a tail for sewing. Stuff very lightly. (photo 19)

Using straight pins, pin the tusks to the underside of the nose between rounds 4-6. (photo 20) You'll want them to be placed further out to the sides, rather than in the center of the nose. With the yarn needle and the tail, sew the tusks to the nose. Secure with a knot and hide inside the nose. (photos 21+22)

REAR FLIPPERS & TAIL

The rear flippers are worked in two pieces. First, crochet one flipper and then join where indicated in the pattern for the second flipper.

Using brown yarn,

R1	Ch 9 then starting in the 2nd ch from the hook and in both loops, leaving the back "bump", sc in each chain across, 8 times. Then turn the work and sc across the back bumps, 8 times. (16 sts) (photos 23-27)
R2	Inc, sc 6, inc in the next two sts, sc 6, inc. (20 sts)
R3	Sc 20.
R4	*Inv dec, sc 8* 2 times. (18 sts)
R5+6	Sc 18.
R7	*Inv dec, sc 7* 2 times. (16 sts)
R8	Sc 16.
R9	*Inv dec, sc 6* 2 times. (14 sts)
R10	*Inv dec, sc 5* 2 times. (12 sts)

Fasten off and leave a tail for sewing. Set aside.

Repeat rounds 1-10 to make a second flipper. Do not fasten off after round 10 and instead, follow the rounds listed on the next page. We're going to connect the flipper pieces and continue working on the tail.

R11	With the second flipper piece still on the hook, insert the hook into the first stitch on the first flipper piece and sc. (photo 28) This will be the stitch to the left of where we fastened off. Sc 12 times total on the first piece. Then, on the second piece, you'll insert the hook into the first stitch of R10 on the second piece. Sc 12 times total on the second piece. (24 sts) (photos 29+30)

Use the yarn needle and the tail left over from the first flipper piece to sew the opening between both pieces closed. (photos 31-33)

R12+13	Sc 24.
R14	*Sc 3, inc* 6 times. (30 sts)
R15	Sc 30.
R16	*Sc 4, inc* 6 times. (36 sts)
R17	Sc 36.
R18	*Sc 5, inc* 6 times. (42 sts)
R19	Sc 42.
R20	*Sc 6, inc* 6 times. (48 sts)
R21	Sc 48.
R22	*Sc 7, inc* 6 times. (54 sts)
R23-25	Sc 54.

Fasten off and leave an extra-long tail for sewing. (photos 34+35)

Add fiberfill to the tail. Make sure to only add fiberfill to the main tail piece, not the flippers. Those will remain unstuffed and flat. Using straight pins, pin the tail to the body between rounds 19-35. (photos 36+37) With the yarn needle and the tail, sew the tail to the body. (photo 38) If needed, add any extra fiberfill to the tail before closing the piece. Secure with a knot and hide inside the body. (photos 39+40)

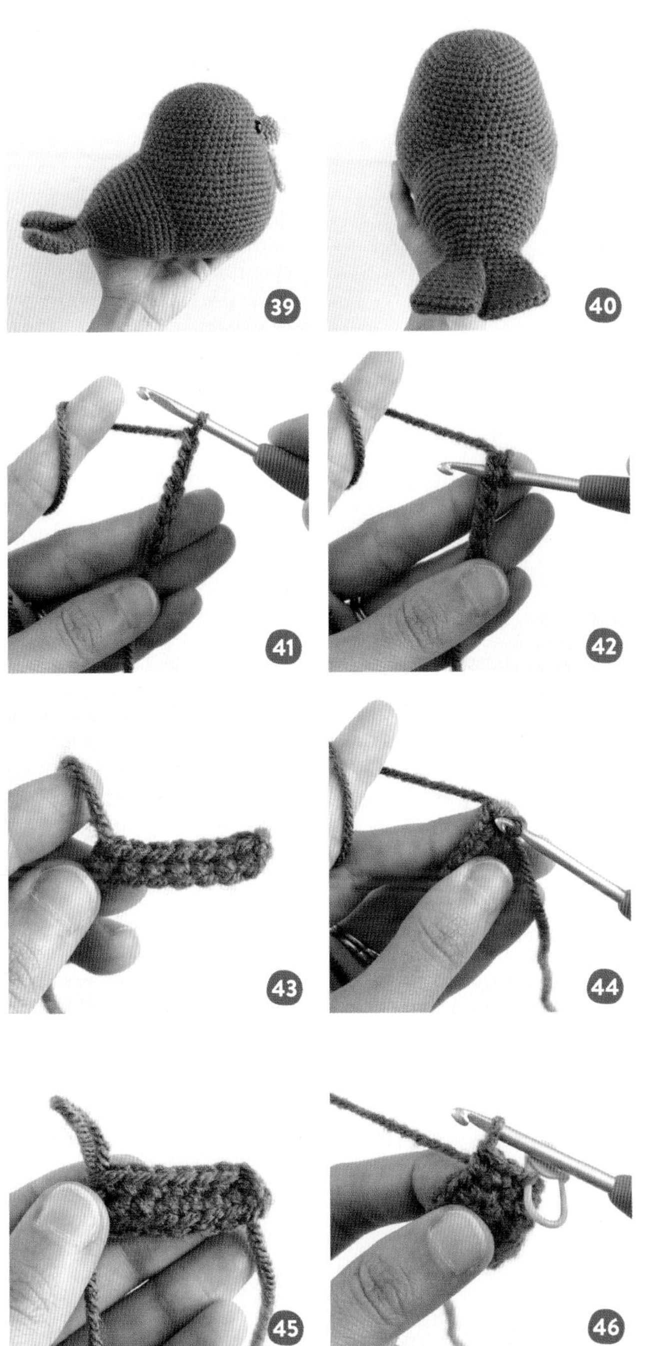

FRONT FLIPPERS: MAKE 2

Using brown yarn,

R1	Ch 8 then starting in the 2nd ch from the hook and in both loops, leaving the back "bump", sc in each chain across, 7 times. Then turn the work and sc across the back bumps, 7 times. (14 sts) (photos 41-45)
R2	*Inc, sc 6* 2 times. (16 sts)
R3	*Inc in the next two sts, sc 6* 2 times. (20 sts)
R4	Sc 2, in FLO sc 10, then sc 8 in both loops as normal. (20 sts) (photos 46-51)
R5	Sc 20.
R6	Sc 1, inv dec, sc 8, inv dec, sc 7. (18 sts)
R7-9	Sc 18.
R10	Sc 1, inv dec, sc 7, inv dec, sc 6. (16 sts)
R11-17	Sc 16.
R18	Sc 4. Next line up the stitches on both sides of the flipper then insert the hook into both stitches. Sc across 7 times. (photos 52-54)

Fasten off and leave a tail for sewing. Leave the flippers unstuffed. (photo 55)

Using straight pins, pin the flippers to the sides of the body between rounds 17-18. (photos 56+57) With the yarn needle and the tail, sew the flippers to the body. Weave the needle under both loops (the "V") from R18 of the flippers and then into the body. (photo 58) Secure with a knot and hide inside the body. (photos 59-61)

47

48

49

50

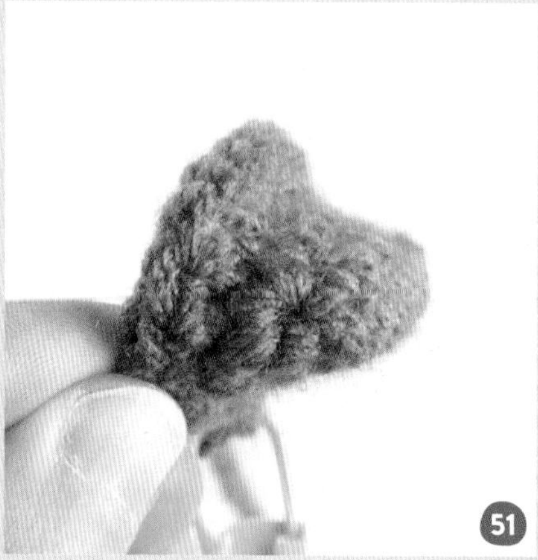

51

52

53

54

55

56

57
58

59

60

61

PETS

CAT

BEGINNER

FINISHED MEASUREMENTS

- Approx. 4 inches wide by 8.5 inches tall by 8 inches long

MATERIALS

- Worsted weight yarn: Light Gray, Dark Gray, White, and Pink
- Size F/3.75mm crochet hook
- One pair of 10.5mm safety eyes
- White embroidery floss and needle
- Polyester fiberfill stuffing
- Yarn needle
- Scissors
- Stitch marker
- Straight pins
- Hot glue gun

ABBREVIATIONS

- Ch- Chain
- Dec- Decrease
- Inc- Increase
- Inv Dec- Invisible Decrease
- R- Round/Row
- Sc- Single Crochet
- St/s- Stitch/es

HEAD

Using light gray yarn,

R1 6 sc in magic ring. (6 sts)
R2 Inc in each st around. (12 sts)
R3 *Sc 1, inc* 6 times. (18 sts)
R4 *Sc 2, inc* 6 times. (24 sts)
R5 *Sc 3, inc* 6 times. (30 sts)
R6 *Sc 4, inc* 6 times. (36 sts)
R7 *Sc 5, inc* 6 times. (42 sts)
R8 *Sc 6, inc* 6 times. (48 sts)
R9 *Sc 7, inc* 6 times. (54 sts)
R10-17 Sc 54.

Add the safety eyes between rounds 14 and 15, placing them about 8 stitches apart.

R18 *Sc 7, inv dec* 6 times. (48 sts)
R19 *Sc 6, inv dec* 6 times. (42 sts)
R20 *Sc 5, inv dec* 6 times. (36 sts)
R21 *Sc 4, inv dec* 6 times. (30 sts)

Begin adding fiberfill and continue adding as you close the piece.

R22 *Sc 3, inv dec* 6 times. (24 sts)
R23 *Sc 2, inv dec* 6 times. (18 sts)
R24 *Sc 1, inv dec* 6 times. (12 sts)
R25 Inv dec around 6 times. (6 sts)

Fasten off and leave a long tail to close the piece and for sewing. The long tail will be used to sew the head to the body. (photo 1)

NOSE

Using white yarn,

R1 6 sc in magic ring. (6 sts)
R2 3 sc into one st, sc 1, 3 sc into one st, sc 1, 3 sc into one st, sc 1. (12 sts)
R3 Sc 1, inc, sc 2, inc, inc, sc 3, inc, sc 2. (16 sts)

Fasten off and leave a tail for sewing. (photo 2)

With pink yarn, sew a nose over round 2. Make a wide "V" then fill in between the two lines until you have a full nose. (photo 3) Stitch one line down the center to the other side of the magic ring. (photo 4) Secure with a knot and trim the end.

For the whiskers, take white embroidery floss and separate it into 3 strands total. Tie a knot at one end and thread the other end onto the needle. Insert the needle from the inside of the nose near round 2 and pull through to the outside. Cut to about 1.5 inches. Make 3 whiskers on each side of the nose. (photo 5) Separate each whisker into 3 strands so it looks fuller.

Using straight pins, pin the nose to the head between rounds 12-17. (photo 6) With the yarn needle and the tail, sew the nose to the head. Weave the needle under both loops (the "V") from the stitches on R3 of the nose and then into the head, coming out through one of the stitch holes. (photo 7) Insert the needle into the same stitch hole and then go over to the next stitch on the nose and repeat. (photo 8) Make sure to go under the stitches and not over them to create a clean finish. Secure with a knot and hide inside the head. (photo 9)

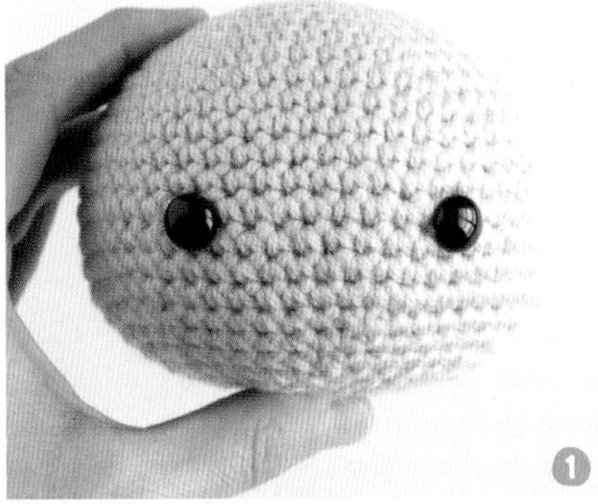

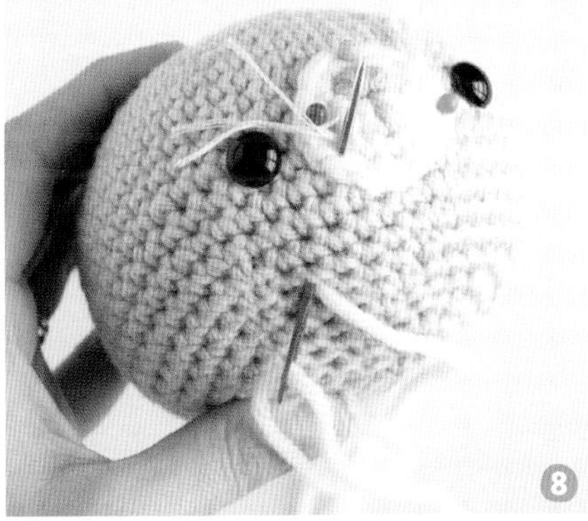

EARS: MAKE 2

Using light gray yarn,

R1	6 sc in magic ring. (6 sts)
R2	*Sc 1, inc* 3 times. (9 sts)
R3	*Sc 2, inc* 3 times. (12 sts)
R4	*Sc 3, inc* 3 times. (15 sts)
R5	*Sc 4, inc* 3 times. (18 sts)
R6	*Sc 5, inc* 3 times. (21 sts)
R7	*Sc 6, inc* 3 times. (24 sts)

Fasten off and leave a tail for sewing. Leave the ears unstuffed. (photo 10)

Using straight pins, pin the ears to the head between rounds 4-12. With the yarn needle and the tail, sew the ears in place. Secure with a knot and hide inside the head. (photos 11-14)

INSIDE OF EARS: MAKE 2

Using pink yarn,

R1	Ch 7 then starting in the 2nd ch from the hook and in both loops, leaving the back "bump", sc in each chain across. (6 sts) Ch 1 and turn. (photos 15-17)
R2	Dec, sc 2, dec. (4 sts) Ch 1 and turn.
R3	Dec 2 times. (2 sts) Ch 1 and turn.
R4	Dec 1 time. (1 st)

Fasten off and leave a tail for sewing. Weave in the starting tail. (photo 18)

Using straight pins, pin the inside pieces to the ears. (photo 19) With the yarn needle and the tail, sew the inside pieces to the ears. Weave the needle into the edge of the inside piece and then into the ear. (photo 20) Pull the needle through both layers of the main ear and come out the back side. (photo 21) Insert the needle into the same stitch hole, weaving through to the front side, and then through the edge of the inside piece. (photos 22+23) This technique makes it so the stitching does not show on the back of the ear. Continue all the way around until you reach the end. Secure with a knot and hide inside the head. (photos 24-26)

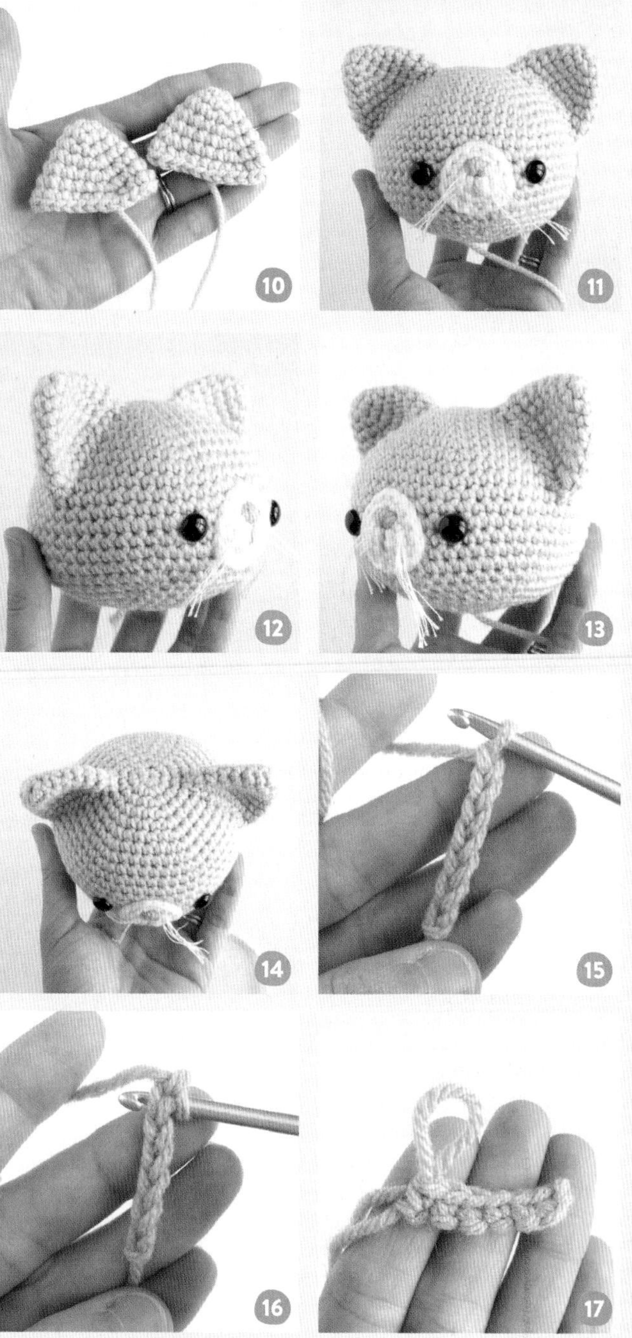

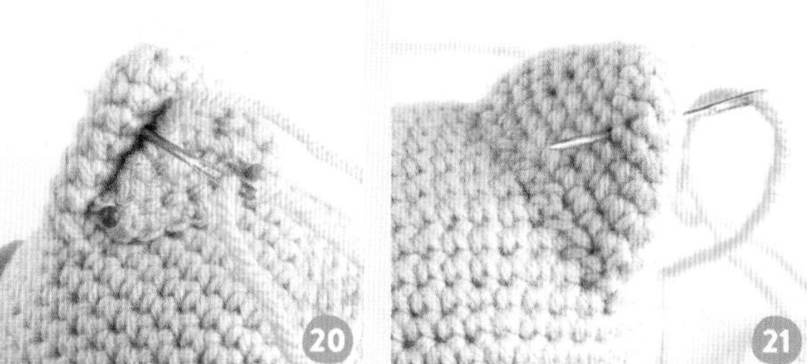

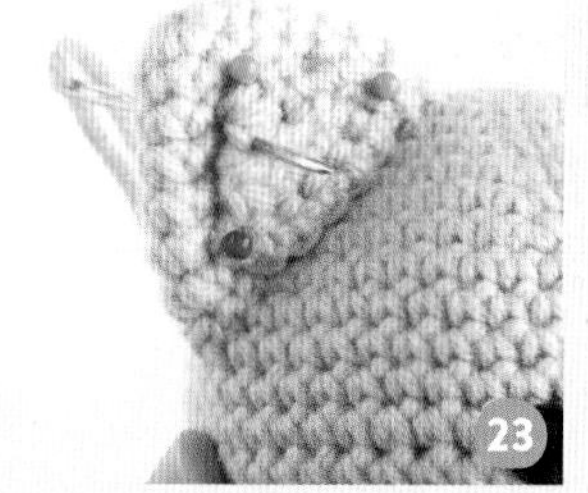

HEAD STRIPES

Use dark gray yarn for all stripes!

FOR TOP OF HEAD

LONG STRIPE: MAKE 1

R1 Ch 18.

Fasten off and leave a tail for sewing. (photo 27)

SHORT STRIPE: MAKE 2

R1 Ch 14.

Fasten off and leave a tail for sewing. (photo 27)

With straight pins, pin the stripes to the top of the head, in between the ears. The long stripe will go in the center. Pin one end starting at R8 on the front of the head then pin the other end near R8 on the back of the head. (photo 28) Repeat for the shorter stripes, placing them at R7 on both sides of the head. (photo 29) Either sew or glue the stripes in place. I prefer to use hot glue for these stripes but do whatever method you prefer. Secure all tails with a knot and hide inside the body. (photos 30-32)

*Photos on next page

SIDES OF HEAD

LONG STRIPE: MAKE 2

R1 Ch 12.

Fasten off and leave a tail for sewing. (photo 33)

SHORT STRIPE: MAKE 2

R1 Ch 8.

Fasten off and leave a tail for sewing. (photo 33)

With straight pins, pin the stripes to the sides of the head. The short stripes will go near round 15 on each side of the head, about 5 stitches away from the eyes. Repeat for the longer stripes, placing them near round 17, about 7 stitches away from the nose. Make sure to center the smaller stripes above the longer ones. (photo 34) Either sew or glue the stripes in place. Again, I prefer to use hot glue for these stripes but do whatever method you prefer. Secure all tails with a knot and hide inside the body. (photos 35-38)

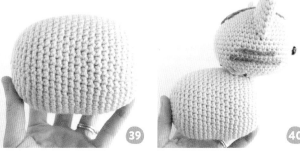

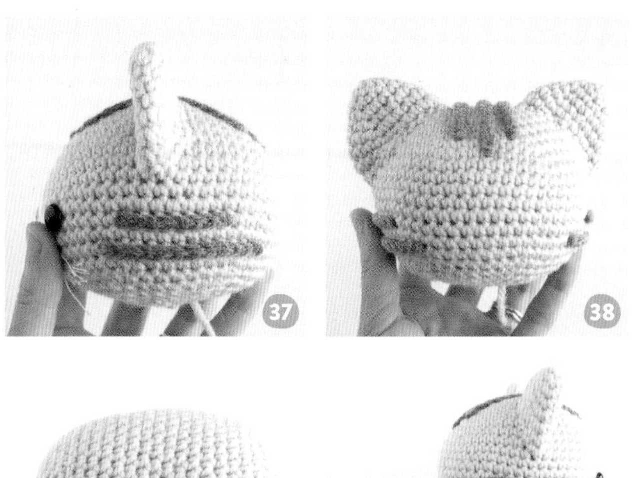

37 38 39 40

41 42

BODY

Using light gray yarn,

R1	6 sc in magic ring. (6 sts)
R2	Inc in each st around. (12 sts)
R3	*Sc 1, inc* 6 times. (18 sts)
R4	*Sc 2, inc* 6 times. (24 sts)
R5	*Sc 3, inc* 6 times. (30 sts)
R6	*Sc 4, inc* 6 times. (36 sts)
R7	*Sc 5, inc* 6 times. (42 sts)
R8-24	Sc 42.
R25	*Sc 5, inv dec* 6 times. (36 sts)
R26	*Sc 4, inv dec* 6 times. (30 sts)

Begin adding fiberfill and continue adding as you close the piece.

R27	*Sc 3, inv dec* 6 times. (24 sts)
R28	*Sc 2, inv dec* 6 times. (18 sts)
R29	*Sc 1, inv dec* 6 times. (12 sts)
R30	Inv dec around 6 times. (6 sts)

Fasten off and leave a tail to close the piece. (photo 39)

Using straight pins, pin the head to the body between rounds 7-12. (photo 40) It's important to place it between these rounds, as it will help balance the cat and keep it on all four legs. Rounds 20-25 of the head will be what is sewn onto the body. With the yarn needle and the tail, weave the needle into the body, then into the head. (photo 41) Repeat all the way around. If needed, sew around the head twice to make sure it is secure and not floppy. Secure with a knot and hide inside the body. (photos 42-44)

43 44

BODY STRIPES: MAKE 4

Using dark gray yarn,

R1 Ch 16.

Fasten off and leave a tail for sewing. (photo 45)

With straight pins, pin the stripes to the top of the body between rounds 16-22. Each stripe should be about 1 round apart. (photos 46+47) Make sure the stripes are centered on the back. Either sew or glue the stripes in place. I prefer to use hot glue for these stripes but do whatever method you prefer. Secure all tails with a knot and hide inside the body. (photos 48+49)

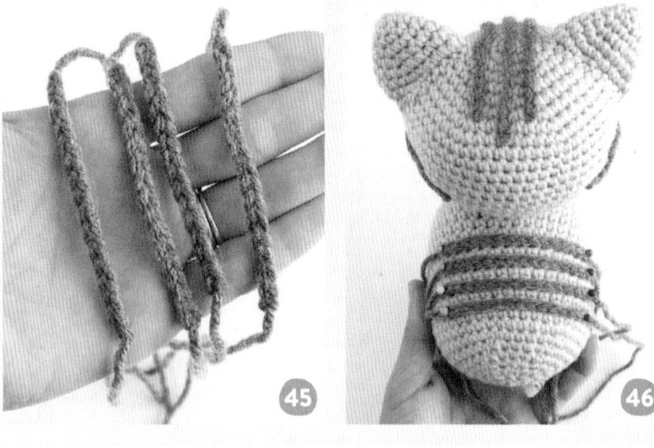

LEGS: MAKE 4

Using pink yarn,

R1 6 sc in magic ring. (6 sts)

R2 Inc in each st around. (12 sts) Fasten off the pink and leave a long tail for the toe pads.

Change to white yarn,

R3 *Sc 1, inc* 6 times. (18 sts)

R4 *Sc 2, inc* 6 times. (24 sts)

R5 Sc 24.

R6 Sc 6, inv dec 6 times, sc 6. (18 sts)

R7 Sc 6, inv dec 3 times, sc 6. (15 sts)

With the yarn needle and the pink yarn tail, make 4 toe pads, stitching over round 4. You'll want the toe pads to be under the decreases from rounds 6 and 7. Go over each spot 3 times to build up a little bump. (photos 50+51) Each pad should be about one stitch apart. Secure with a knot and hide inside the leg. (photo 52)

R8 Sc 15.

Change to light gray yarn,

Begin adding fiberfill and continue adding as you work the piece.

R9-15 Sc 15.

Fasten off and leave a tail for sewing. (photo 53)

Using straight pins, pin the legs to the body. Place the front legs between rounds 9-14, about 1 to 2 stitches apart. (photos 54+55) With the yarn needle and the tail, sew the legs into place on the body. (photos 56+57) Then place the back legs between rounds 20-25, about 1 to 2 stitches apart and sew into place. (photo 58) Secure with a knot and hide inside the body. (photos 59+60)

TAIL

Note: There are several color changes for this part of the pattern. When changing colors, simply drop the old color, pick up the new color, and continue crocheting as normal. This pattern is written so that when there is a color change, all you have to do is carry the yarn up the couple of rounds where it was last dropped.

Using dark gray yarn,

R1	7 sc in magic ring. (7 sts)
R2	Inc in each st around. (14 sts)
R3-5	Sc 14.

Change to light gray yarn,

R6-8 Sc 14.

Change to dark gray yarn,

R9+10 Sc 14.

Change to light gray yarn,

R11-13 Sc 14.

Begin adding fiberfill and continue adding as you work the piece.

Change to dark gray yarn,

R14+15 Sc 14.

Change to light gray yarn,

R16-18 Sc 14.

Change to dark gray yarn,

R19+20 Sc 14.

Change to light gray yarn and fasten off the dark gray yarn,

R21-23 Sc 14.

Fasten off and leave a tail for sewing. (photo 61)

Using straight pins, pin the tail to the body between rounds 24-28. (photos 62+63) With the yarn needle and the tail, sew the tail to the body. Secure with a knot and hide inside the body. To finish, bend the tip of the tail at rounds 9 and 10. No pipe cleaner or craft wire is required for the tail to bend. (photos 64-66)

61

62

63

64

65

66

CHAMELEON

EXPERT

FINISHED MEASUREMENTS

- Approx. 3.5 inches wide by 4 inches tall by 8 inches long

MATERIALS

- Worsted weight yarn: Lime Green, Aqua, and White
- Size F/3.75mm crochet hook
- One pair of 8mm safety eyes
- Black embroidery floss and needle
- Polyester fiberfill stuffing
- Yarn needle
- Scissors
- Stitch marker
- Straight pins
- Pipe Cleaner: 2 pieces measuring 9 inches long and 4 pieces measuring 6 inches long

ABBREVIATIONS

- Inc- Increase
- Inv Dec- Invisible Decrease
- R- Round/Row
- Sc- Single Crochet
- St/s- Stitch/es

Note: The chameleon body has a lot of color changes. I found it best to cut the yarn after each color change and rejoin it when needed. Just make sure to secure all the ends if you do this method. Another option is to carry the yarn behind the work and pick it up when needed. I didn't like this method, as the yarn being carried was visible through the stitches. Remember to leave loose tension on the color not being used if you do this method.

HEAD

Using lime green yarn,

R1 6 sc in magic ring. (6 sts)
R2 Inc in each st around. (12 sts)
R3 *Sc 1, inc* 6 times. (18 sts)
R4 Sc 18.
R5 *Sc 2, inc* 6 times. (24 sts)
R6 Sc 24.
R7 *Sc 3, inc* 6 times. (30 sts)
R8 Sc 30.
R9 *Sc 4, inc* 6 times. (36 sts)
R10 Sc 36.
R11 *Sc 5, inc* 6 times. (42 sts)
R12 Sc 15, inc in the next 12 sts, sc 15. (54 sts) (photos 1+2)
R13 Sc 54.
R14 Sc 15, inv dec 12 times, sc 15. (42 sts) (photos 3+4)
R15 *Sc 5, inv dec* 6 times. (36 sts)
R16 *Sc 4, inv dec* 6 times. (30 sts)
R17 *Sc 3, inv dec* 6 times. (24 sts)

Begin adding fiberfill and continue adding as you close the piece.

R18 *Sc 2, inv dec* 6 times. (18 sts)
R19 *Sc 1, inv dec* 6 times. (12 sts)
R20 Inv dec around 6 times. (6 sts)

Fasten off and leave a tail to close the piece. (photos 5+6)

EYES: MAKE 2

Using white yarn,

R1	6 sc in magic ring. (6 sts)
R2	Inc in each st around. (12 sts)
R3	Sc 12.

Fasten off and leave a tail for sewing.

Add the safety eyes in the center of the magic ring and attach the safety backings. (photo 7) Using straight pins, pin the eyes to the head between rounds 7-11. (photo 8) The eyes should be about 12 stitches apart when counting between rounds 8 and 9. With the yarn needle and the tail, sew the eyes in place on the head. (photo 9) No fiberfill will be added to the eyes. Secure with a knot and hide inside the head. (photos 10-12)

With black embroidery floss, add a mouth to the head. Start near R5 on one side of the magic ring, then insert the needle into the head near R5 on the other side of the magic ring. You can either have the thread go straight across or you can pull it down just a little bit to form a wide U and make a smile. Secure with a knot and hide inside the head. (photos 13+14)

BODY

With the two pipe cleaner pieces measuring 9 inches long, twist together to form one pipe cleaner. Set aside until after round 8. (photos 15+16)

Using lime green yarn,

R1	6 sc in magic ring. (6 sts)
R2-30	Sc 6. After R8 insert the pipe cleaner into the tail and continue to crochet each round. (photo 17)
R31	*Sc 1, inc* 3 times. (9 sts)
R32	*Sc 2, inc* 3 times. (12 sts)
R33	Sc 12.
R34	*Sc 3, inc* 3 times. (15 sts)
R35	*Sc 4, inc* 3 times. (18 sts) (photo 18)

R36 With lime green *sc 2, inc* 2 times, sc 2, with aqua inc, sc 2, inc, with lime green *sc 2, inc* 2 times. (24 sts)

R37 With lime green sc 24.

R38 With lime green *sc 3, inc* 2 times, sc 3, with aqua inc, sc 3, inc, with lime green *sc 3, inc* 2 times. (30 sts)

R39 With lime green *sc 4, inc* 6 times. (36 sts)

R40 With lime green *sc 5, inc* 2 times, sc 3, with aqua sc 2, inc, sc 5, inc, sc, with lime green sc 4, inc, sc 5, inc. (42 sts)

R41 With lime green sc 42.

R42 With lime green sc 17, with aqua sc 13, with lime green sc 12. (42 sts)

R43 With lime green sc 42.

R44 With lime green sc 17, with aqua sc 14, with lime green sc 11. (42 sts)

R45 With lime green sc 42.

R46 With lime green sc 17, with aqua sc 15, with lime green sc 10. (42 sts)

R47 With lime green sc 42.

R48 With lime green sc 17, with aqua sc 16, with lime green sc 9. (42 sts)

R49 With lime green *sc 5, inv dec* 6 times. (36 sts)

R50 With lime green sc 16, with aqua sc 12, with lime green sc 8. (36 sts)

Begin adding fiberfill and continue adding as you work the piece.

R51 With lime green *sc 4, inv dec* 6 times. (30 sts)

R52 With lime green sc 15, with aqua sc 8, with lime green sc 7. (30 sts)

R53 With lime green *sc 3, inv dec* 6 times. (24 sts)

R54 With lime green sc 13, with aqua sc 6, with lime green sc 5. (24 sts) Fasten off the aqua yarn and secure with a knot.

Continuing with lime green yarn,

R55+56 Sc 24.

Fasten off and leave a tail for sewing. (photo 19)

Starting at the tip of the tail, curl up toward the body. (photos 20-23) Using straight pins, pin the body to the back of the head, near round 18. (photos 24+25) With the yarn needle and the tail, sew the body to the head. Secure with a knot and hide inside the body. (photos 26+27)

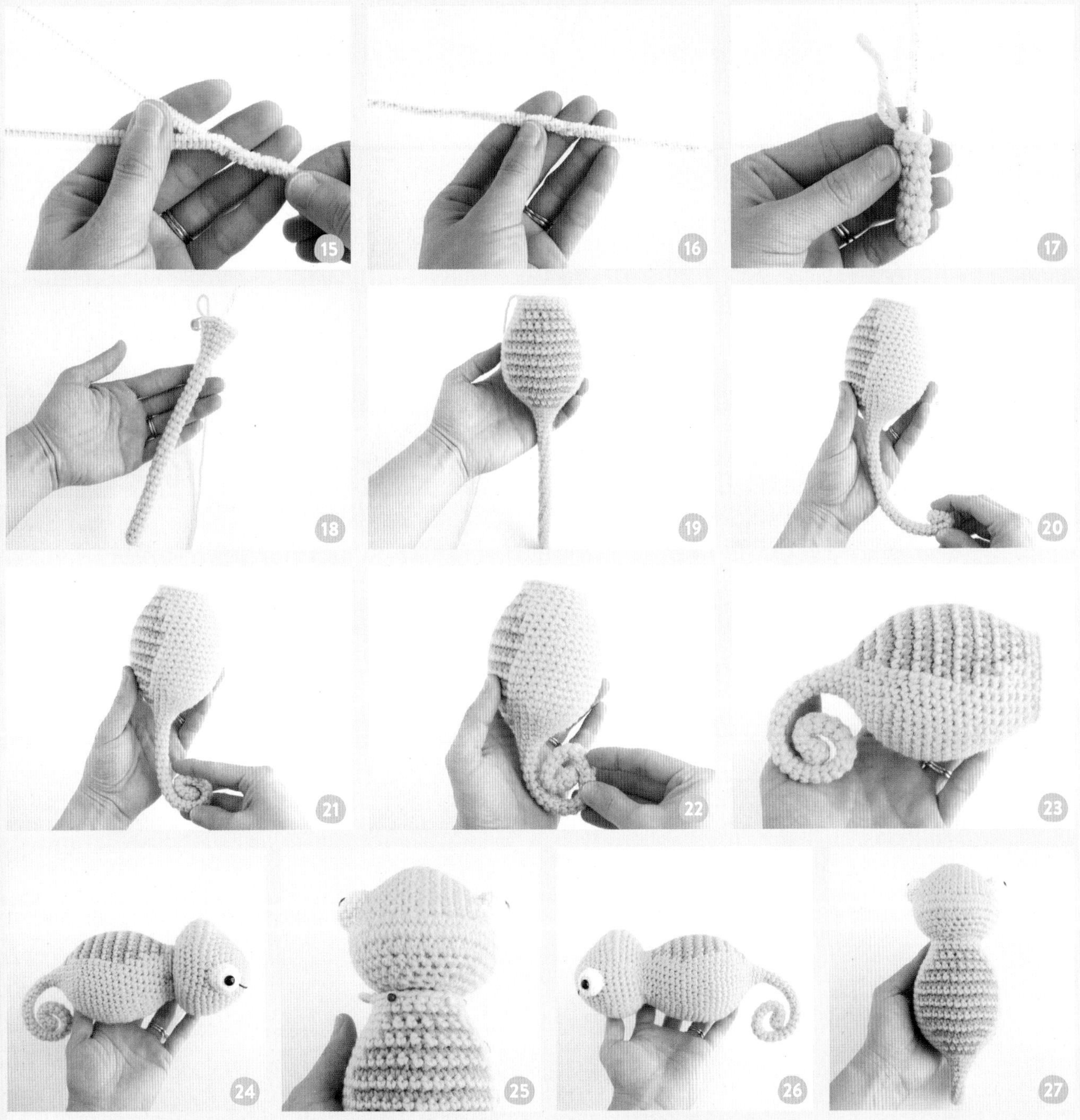
15
16
17
18
19
20
21
22
23
24
25
26
27

LEGS: MAKE 4

First, we're going to shape the pipe cleaners that will go inside of the toes and legs. Take one 6-inch pipe cleaner and fold one inch at the end. (photo 28) Then fold the pipe cleaner up one inch, then down one inch again. (photos 29+30) This will create an "M" shape. Separate the "M" to form a "V". Each side of the "V" will slide into each toe. With the remaining pipe cleaner, wrap it around the center twice. (photo 31) Leave the remaining length of pipe cleaner for the leg. (photo 32)

The toes are worked in two pieces. First, crochet one toe and then join where indicated in the pattern for the second toe.

Using lime green yarn,

R1 6 sc in magic ring. (6 sts)

R2+3 Sc 6.

Fasten off and leave a tail for sewing. Set aside (photo 33)

Repeat rounds 1-3 to make a second toe. Do not fasten off after round 3 and instead, follow the rounds listed below. We're going to connect the pieces and continue working on the leg.

R4 With the second toe still on the hook, insert the hook into the first stitch on the first toe piece and sc. This will be the stitch to the left of where we fastened off. (photos 34+35) Sc 6 times total on the first piece. Then on the second piece, you'll insert the hook into the first stitch we made in R3 for the second toe piece. (photo 36) Sc 6 times total on the second piece. (12 sts) (photo 37)

Use the yarn needle and the tail left over from the first toe piece to sew the opening between both pieces closed. (photo 38)

R5 *Sc 1, inv dec* 4 times. (8 sts) (photo 39)

Take the pipe cleaner and insert each side into the toes. Continue crocheting around the pipe cleaner as you work the next rounds. (photos 40+41)

R6-10 Sc 8.

Fasten off and leave a tail for sewing. Leave the legs unstuffed. A little bit of pipe cleaner will stick out the top of the leg, this part will be inserted into the body. (photo 42) Finally, bend where the leg and toes come together. (photo 43)

Repeat 3 more times until you have 4 legs total. (photo 44)

Place the front legs between rounds 48-50. Using a chopstick or the end of a crochet hook, make a hole in the body so the pipe cleaner can be easily inserted. (photos 45+46) The front legs should be about 4 to 5 stitches apart. (photo 47) With the yarn needle and the tail, sew the legs into place on the body. (photo 48) Repeat for the back legs, placing them between rounds 40-42, about 4 to 5 stitches apart. (photo 49) Sew into place. Secure all tails with a knot and hide inside the body. (photos 50-52)

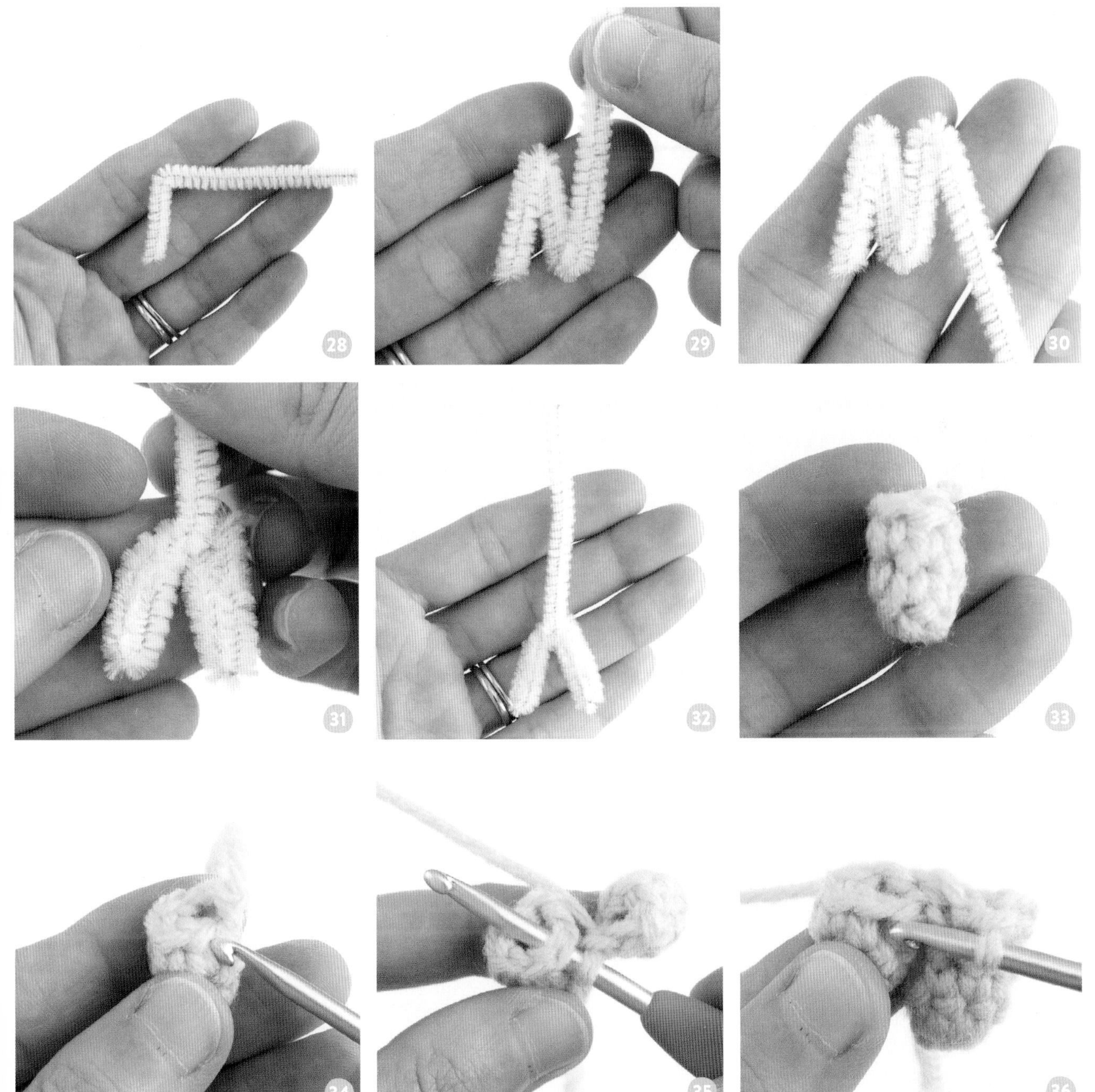
28
29
30
31
32
33
34
35
36

37  38  39

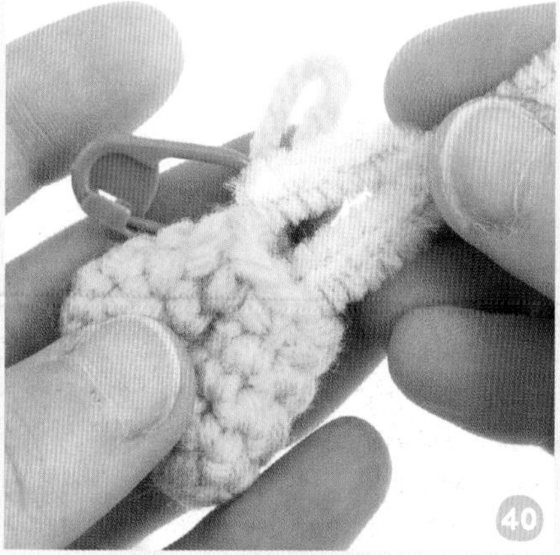

40  41  42

43  44 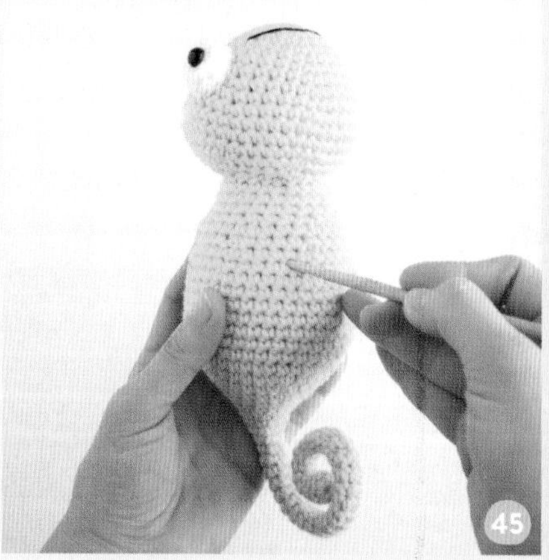 45

46
47
48
49
50
51
52

COCKATIEL

BEGINNER

FINISHED MEASUREMENTS

- Approx. 5 inches wide by 5.5 inches tall

MATERIALS

- Worsted weight yarn: Light Yellow, Dark Gray, Orange, and Peach
- Size F/3.75mm crochet hook
- One pair of 10mm safety eyes
- Polyester fiberfill stuffing
- Yarn needle
- Scissors
- Stitch marker
- Straight pins

ABBREVIATIONS

- Ch- Chain
- Dc- Double Crochet
- Hdc- Half Double Crochet
- Inc- Increase
- Inv Dec- Invisible Decrease
- R- Round/Row
- Sc- Single Crochet
- St/s- Stitch/es

FACE SPOTS: MAKE 2

Using orange yarn,

R1	6 sc in magic ring. (6 sts)

Fasten off and leave a tail for sewing. Set aside. (photo 1)

BODY

With light yellow yarn,

R1	6 sc in magic ring. (6 sts)
R2	Inc in each st around. (12 sts)
R3	*Sc 1, inc* 6 times. (18 sts)
R4	*Sc 2, inc* 6 times. (24 sts)
R5	*Sc 3, inc* 6 times. (30 sts)
R6	*Sc 4, inc* 6 times. (36 sts)
R7	*Sc 5, inc* 6 times. (42 sts)
R8-10	Sc 42.
R11	*Sc 13, inc* 3 times. (45 sts)
R12	*Sc 14, inc* 3 times. (48 sts)
R13	*Sc 7, inc* 6 times. (54 sts)
R14	*Sc 7, inv dec* 6 times. (48 sts)
R15	*Sc 6, inv dec* 6 times. (42 sts)
R16	Sc 42.

Add the safety eyes between rounds 11 and 12, placing them about 7 stitches apart.

With peach yarn, sew a beak in between the eyes between rounds 10-13. First start with the vertical lines by making a wide "V". (photo 2) Then fill in between the two lines until you have a full beak. Make about 9 to 10 lines to build up the beak. These lines should span over 4 stitches. (photo 3) Next, create the horizontal lines, starting at one side of the vertical lines and going over to the other side. Make about 3 to 4 lines to cover the tops of the vertical lines. (photo 4) Secure with a knot and trim the end. Next add the face spots. Position them on the sides of the body between rounds 13-15. (photo 5) With the yarn needle and the tail, sew the face spots to the body. Weave the needle under both loops (the "V") from R1 of the face spots and then into the

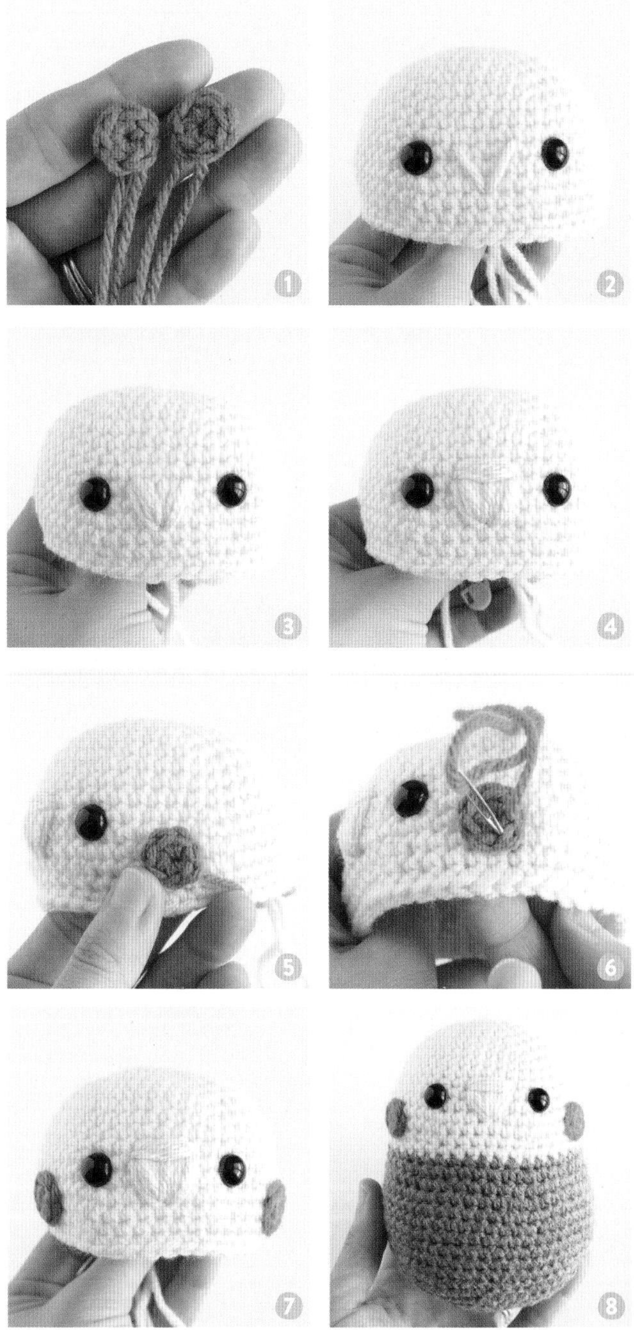

body. (photo 6) Continue all the way around. Secure with a knot and hide inside the body. (photo 7)

Change to dark gray yarn,

R17	Sc 42.
R18	*Sc 6, inc* 6 times. (48 sts)
R19	Sc 48.
R20	*Sc 7, inc* 6 times. (54 sts)
R21-26	Sc 54.
R27	*Sc 7, inv dec* 6 times. (48 sts)
R28	Sc 48.
R29	*Sc 6, inv dec* 6 times. (42 sts)
R30	*Sc 5, inv dec* 6 times. (36 sts)

Begin adding fiberfill and continue adding as you close the piece.

R31	*Sc 4, inv dec* 6 times. (30 sts)
R32	*Sc 3, inv dec* 6 times. (24 sts)
R33	*Sc 2, inv dec* 6 times. (18 sts)
R34	*Sc 1, inv dec* 6 times. (12 sts)
R35	Inv dec around 6 times. (6 sts)

Fasten off and leave a tail to close the piece. (photos 8-10)

WINGS: MAKE 2

Using dark gray yarn,

R1	6 sc in magic ring. (6 sts)
R2	Inc in each st around. (12 sts)
R3	Sc 12.
R4	*Sc 1, inc* 6 times. (18 sts)
R5	Sc 18.
R6	*Sc 2, inc* 6 times. (24 sts)
R7+8	Sc 24.
R9	*Sc 2, inv dec* 6 times. (18 sts)
R10	Sc 18.
R11	*Sc 1, inv dec* 6 times. (12 sts)
R12	Sc 5. Do this by lining up the stitches on both sides of the wing, then inserting the hook into both stitches. Then sc as normal. (photos 11-14)

Fasten off and leave a tail for sewing. Leave the wings unstuffed. (photo 15)

Using straight pins, pin the wings to the sides of the body near round 17. (photos 16+17) With the yarn needle and the tail, sew the wings to the body. Weave the needle under both loops (the "V") from R12 of the wings and then into the body. (photos 18-20) Secure with a knot and hide inside the body. (photos 21-23)

HAIR PIECES

Use light yellow yarn for all pieces!

LARGE: MAKE 1

R1 Ch 8 then starting in the 2nd ch from the hook, hdc in the next two chain spaces, dc in the next five chain spaces. (7 sts) (photos 24-26)

Fasten off and leave a tail for sewing.

MEDIUM: MAKE 3

R1 Ch 6 then starting in the 2nd ch from the hook, hdc in the next two chain spaces, dc in the next three chain spaces. (5 sts)

Fasten off and leave a tail for sewing. (photo 27)

SMALL: MAKE 2

R1 Ch 4 then starting in the 2nd ch from the hook, hdc, dc in the next two chain spaces. (3 sts)

Fasten off and leave a tail for sewing. (photo 28)

Use straight pins when positioning the hair feathers. Sew each feather into place after it is pinned, as this is much easier than having to sew when all the feathers are pinned into place.

The large piece will go near round 5. (photos 29-31) For the medium pieces, place two side by side right behind the large piece. (photo 32) Place the last medium piece near rounds 3 and 4, behind the two medium pieces. (photo 33) Then, for the two small pieces, place side by side right behind the single medium piece. (photo 34) For the starting tail, weave in and secure with a knot. Secure all tails with a knot and hide inside the body. (photos 35-37)

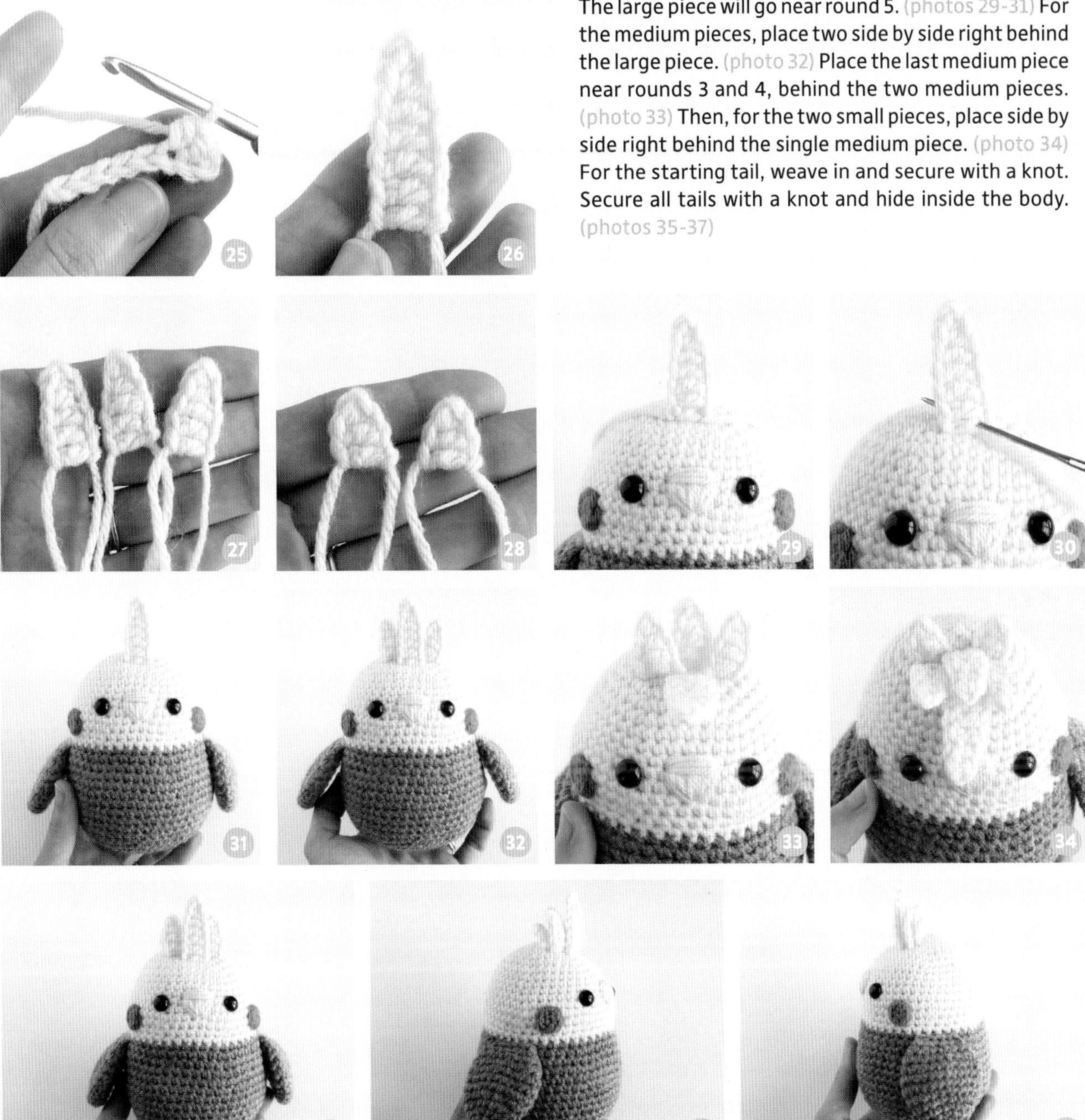

TAIL FEATHERS: MAKE 3

Using dark gray yarn,

R1	6 sc in magic ring. (6 sts)
R2	Inc in each st around. (12 sts)
R3	Sc 12.
R4	*Sc 1, inv dec* 4 times. (8 sts)
R5-11	Sc 8.

Fasten off and leave a tail for sewing. Leave the feathers unstuffed. (photo 38)

Using straight pins, pin two feathers in the center of the body near round 26. (photo 39) With the yarn needle and the tail, sew the feathers into place. Take the last feather and pin it in the center, underneath the two top feathers, near round 29. (photo 40) Use the yarn needle to sew into place. Secure the ends with a knot and hide inside the body. (photos 41+42)

FEET: MAKE 2

Using peach yarn,

R1 Ch 7 then starting in the 2nd ch from the hook and in both loops, leaving the back "bump", sc in the next 3 chain spaces, then ch 4. In the 2nd ch from the hook and in both loops, leaving the back "bump" again, sc in the next 3 chain spaces. Sc in the remaining 3 chain spaces on the main chain piece. (9 sts) (photos 43-49)

Fasten off and leave a tail for sewing. (photo 50)

Using straight pins, pin the feet to the body near round 32, placing them about 4 to 5 stitches apart. (photo 51) With the yarn needle and the tail, sew the feet into place on the body. (photo 52) Secure all tails with a knot and hide inside the body. (photos 53-56)

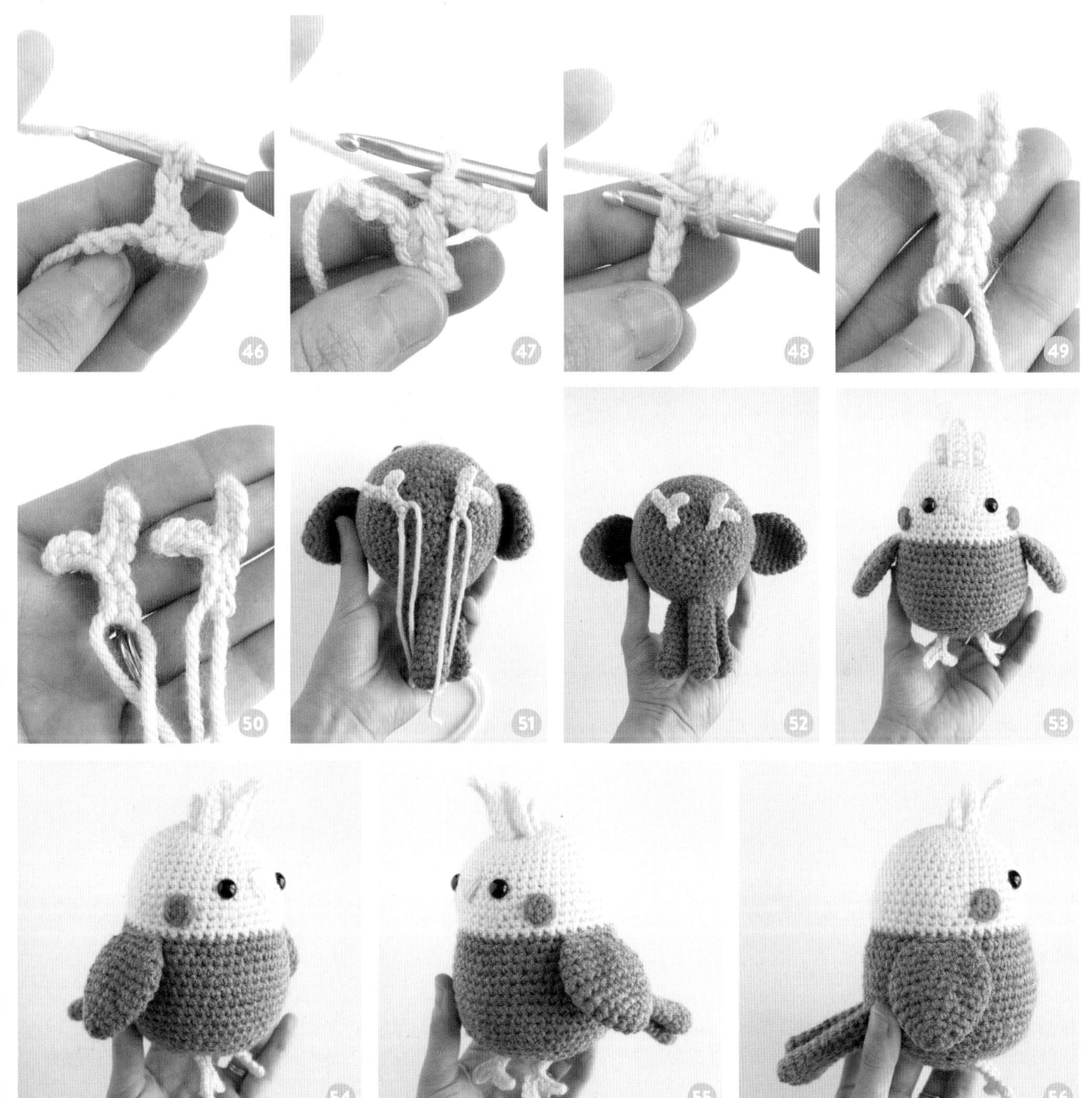
46
47
48
49
50
51
52
53
54
55
56

DOG

BEGINNER

FINISHED MEASUREMENTS

- Approx. 5 inches wide by 8 inches tall by 8 inches long

MATERIALS

- Worsted weight yarn: Tan, Dark Brown, Cream, Red, and Gold
- Size F/3.75mm crochet hook
- One pair of 10.5mm safety eyes
- Polyester fiberfill stuffing
- Yarn needle
- Scissors
- Stitch marker
- Straight pins
- Optional: Hot glue gun

ABBREVIATIONS

- Ch- Chain
- Dc- Double Crochet
- Hdc- Half Double Crochet
- Inc- Increase
- Inv Dec- Invisible Decrease
- R- Round/Row
- Sc- Single Crochet
- St/s- Stitch/es

EYE PATCH

Using dark brown yarn,

R1	6 sc in magic ring. (6 sts)
R2	Inc in each st around. (12 sts)
R3	*Sc 1, inc* 6 times. (18 sts)
R4	Sc 3, inc in the next four sts, sc 11. (22 sts)

Fasten off and leave a tail for sewing.

Insert one of the safety eyes between rounds 1 and 2. Do not attach the safety backing yet. Set aside. (photo 1)

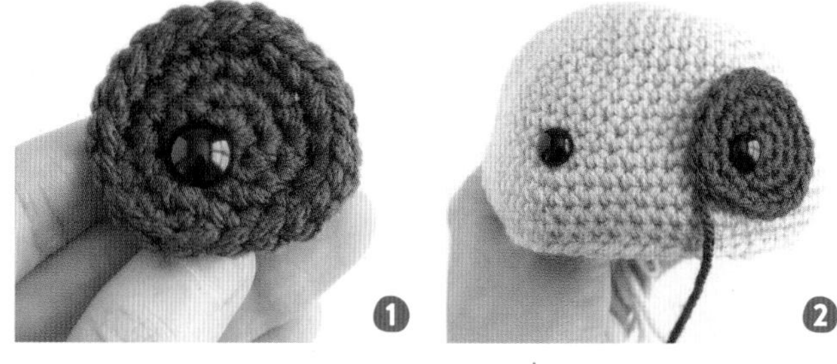

HEAD

Using tan yarn,

R1	6 sc in magic ring. (6 sts)
R2	Inc in each st around. (12 sts)
R3	*Sc 1, inc* 6 times. (18 sts)
R4	*Sc 2, inc* 6 times. (24 sts)
R5	*Sc 3, inc* 6 times. (30 sts)
R6	*Sc 4, inc* 6 times. (36 sts)
R7	*Sc 5, inc* 6 times. (42 sts)
R8	*Sc 6, inc* 6 times. (48 sts)
R9	*Sc 7, inc* 6 times. (54 sts)
R10-15	Sc 54.
R16	*Sc 8, inc* 6 times. (60 sts)
R17	*Sc 9, inc* 6 times. (66 sts)
R18	Sc 66.
R19	*Sc 9, inv dec* 6 times. (60 sts)
R20	*Sc 8, inv dec* 6 times. (54 sts)
R21	*Sc 7, inv dec* 6 times. (48 sts)

Add the safety eyes between rounds 15 and 16, placing them about 8 stitches apart. (photo 2) With the yarn needle and the tail for the eye patch, sew the patch into place, at an angle, onto the head. The patch should lie between rounds 11-18. Weave the needle under both loops (the "V") from R4 of the eye patch and then into the head. (photos 3+4) Continue all the way around the patch. Secure with a knot and hide inside the head. (photo 5)

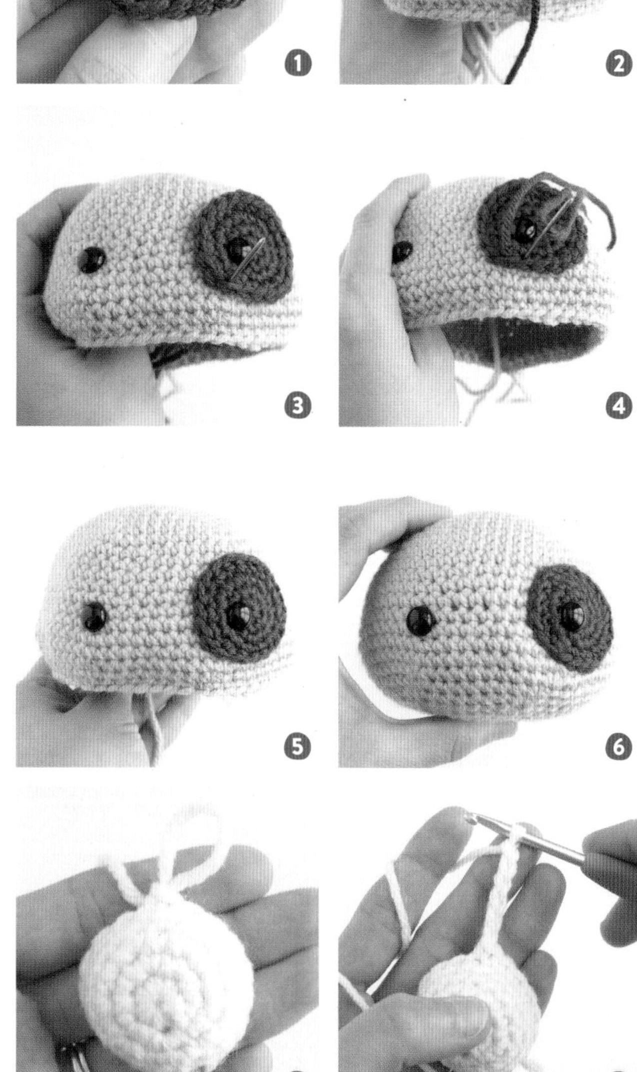

R22	*Sc 6, inv dec* 6 times. (42 sts)
R23	*Sc 5, inv dec* 6 times. (36 sts)
R24	*Sc 4, inv dec* 6 times. (30 sts)

Begin adding fiberfill and continue adding as you close the piece.

R25	*Sc 3, inv dec* 6 times. (24 sts)
R26	*Sc 2, inv dec* 6 times. (18 sts)
R27	*Sc 1, inv dec* 6 times. (12 sts)
R28	Inv dec around 6 times. (6 sts)

Fasten off and leave a long tail to close the piece and for sewing. The long tail will be used to sew the head to the body. (photo 6)

SNOUT

Using cream yarn,

R1	6 sc in magic ring. (6 sts)
R2	Inc in each st around. (12 sts)
R3	*Sc 1, inc* 6 times. (18 sts)
R4+5	Sc 18. (photo 7)
R6	Sc 8, ch 6 then starting in the 2nd ch from the hook, sc, hdc, dc in the next three chain spaces. (photos 8-10) Skip 1 stitch (this will be the stitch right after the 8th sc) and sc 9. (22 sts) (photos 11-13)

Fasten off and leave a tail for sewing. (photo 14)

With dark brown yarn, stitch the nose over round 3, spanning 5 stitches in length. (photo 15) Go over the spot about 8 times to build up the nose. (photo 16) Stitch one line down to the center of the magic ring. Secure with a knot and hide inside the snout. (photo 17)

Using straight pins, pin the snout between rounds 13-19. (photo 18) The strip should point toward the top of the head and will stop at round 8. The snout will overlap the eye patch by just a little bit. (photo 19) With the yarn needle and the tail, sew the snout and strip into place on the head. (photos 20+21) Make sure to sew the skipped stitch from round 6 to the head as well. Add fiberfill to the snout before closing the piece. Secure with a knot and hide inside the head. (photo 22)

EARS: MAKE 2

Using dark brown yarn,

R1	Ch 8 then starting in the 2nd ch from the hook and in both loops, leaving the back "bump", sc in each chain across, 7 times. Then turn the work and sc across the back bumps, 7 times. (14 sts) (photos 23-27)
R2	Inc, sc 5, inc in the next two sts, sc 5, inc. (18 sts)
R3	Inc in the next two sts, sc 6, inc in the next three sts, sc 6, inc. (24 sts)
R4+5	Sc 24.
R6	*Inv dec, sc 10* 2 times. (22 sts)
R7	*Inv dec, sc 9* 2 times. (20 sts)
R8+9	Sc 20.
R10	*Inv dec, sc 8* 2 times. (18 sts)
R11+12	Sc 18.
R13	*Inv dec, sc 7* 2 times. (16 sts)

R14+15	Sc 16.
R16	Sc 1. Next line up the stitches on both sides of the ear then insert the hook into both stitches. Sc across 7 times. (photos 28-31)

Fasten off and leave a tail for sewing. Leave the ears unstuffed. (photo 32)

Using straight pins, pin the ears to the head near round 5. (photo 33) With the yarn needle and the tail, sew the ears to the head. Weave the needle under both loops (the "V") from R16 of the ear and then into the head. (photos 34 +35) Secure with a knot and hide inside the head. (photos 36-39)

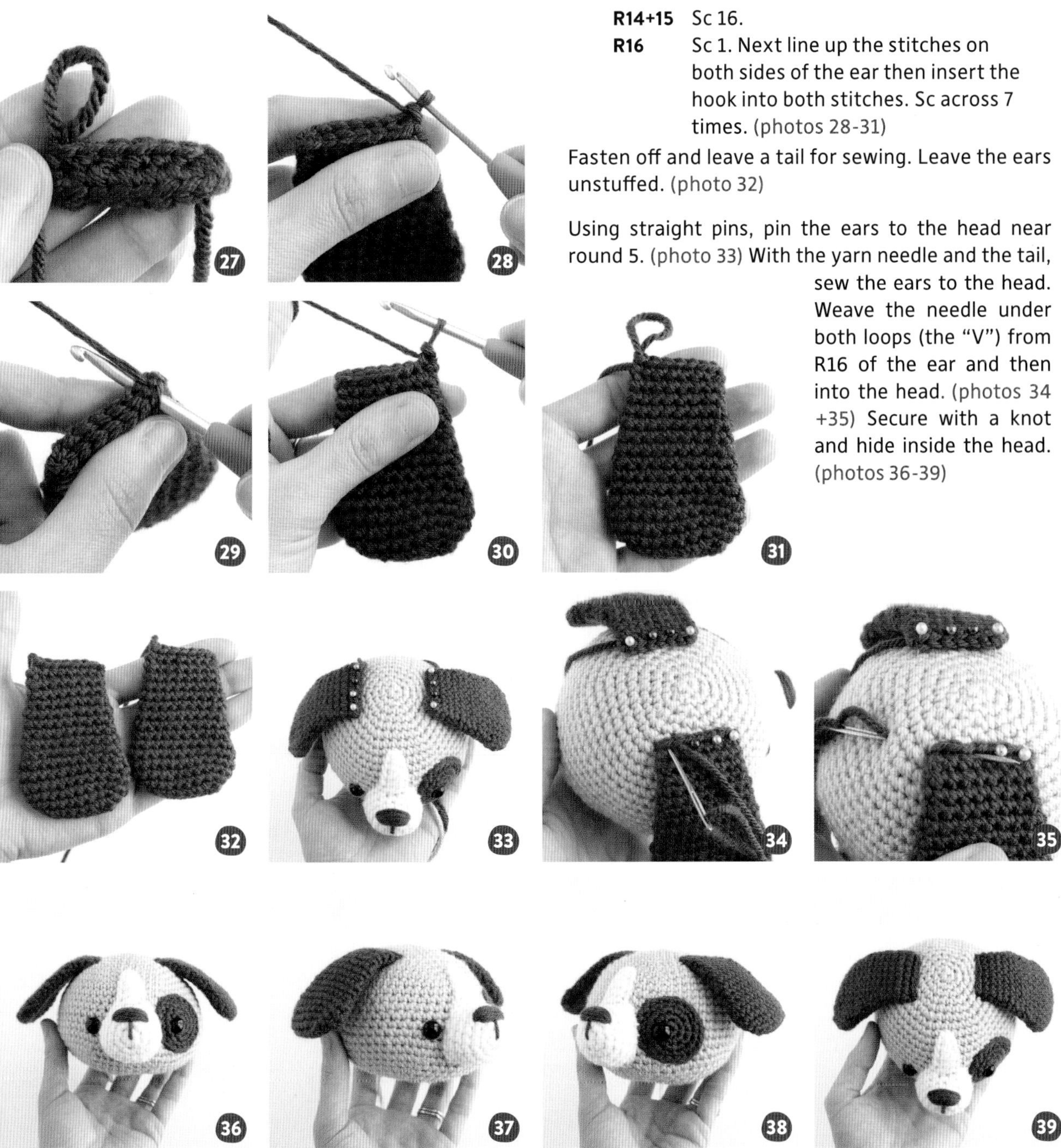

BODY

Using tan yarn,

R1	6 sc in magic ring. (6 sts)
R2	Inc in each st around. (12 sts)
R3	*Sc 1, inc* 6 times. (18 sts)
R4	*Sc 2, inc* 6 times. (24 sts)
R5	*Sc 3, inc* 6 times. (30 sts)
R6	*Sc 4, inc* 6 times. (36 sts)
R7	*Sc 5, inc* 6 times. (42 sts)
R8-29	Sc 42.
R30	*Sc 5, inv dec* 6 times. (36 sts)
R31	*Sc 4, inv dec* 6 times. (30 sts)

Begin adding fiberfill and continue adding as you close the piece.

R32	*Sc 3, inv dec* 6 times. (24 sts)
R33	*Sc 2, inv dec* 6 times. (18 sts)
R34	*Sc 1, inv dec* 6 times. (12 sts)
R35	Inv dec around 6 times. (6 sts)

Fasten off and leave a tail to close the piece. (photo 40)

Using straight pins, pin the head to the body between rounds 8-15. (photo 41) It's important to place it between these rounds, as it will help balance the dog and keep it on all four legs. Rounds 24-28 of the head will be sewn onto the body. With the yarn needle, weave it into the body then into the head. (photo 42) Repeat all the way around. If needed, sew around the head twice to make sure it is secure and not floppy. Secure with a knot and hide inside the body. (photos 43+44)

LEGS: MAKE 4

Using dark brown yarn,

R1	6 sc in magic ring. (6 sts)
R2	Inc in each st around. (12 sts) Fasten off the dark brown and leave a long tail for the toe pads. (photo 45)

Change to tan yarn,

R3	*Sc 1, inc* 6 times. (18 sts)
R4	*Sc 2, inc* 6 times. (24 sts)
R5+6	Sc 24.
R7	Sc 6, inv dec 6 times, sc 6. (18 sts)
R8	Sc 6, inv dec 3 times, sc 6. (15 sts)

With the yarn needle and the dark brown yarn tail, make 4 toe pads, stitching over round 4. You'll want the toe pads to be under the decreases from rounds 7 and 8. Go over each spot 3 times to build up a little bump. Each pad should be about one stitch apart. Secure with a knot and hide inside the leg. (photos 46+47)

Begin adding fiberfill and continue adding as you work the piece.

R9-16	Sc 15.

Fasten off and leave a tail for sewing. (photo 48)

Using straight pins, pin the legs to the body. Place the front legs between rounds 11-17, about 1 to 2 stitches apart. (photo 49) With the yarn needle and the tail, sew the legs into place on the body. (photos 50+51) Then place the back legs between rounds 23-29, about 1 to 2 stitches apart and sew into place. (photo 52) Secure with a knot and hide inside the body. (photo 53)

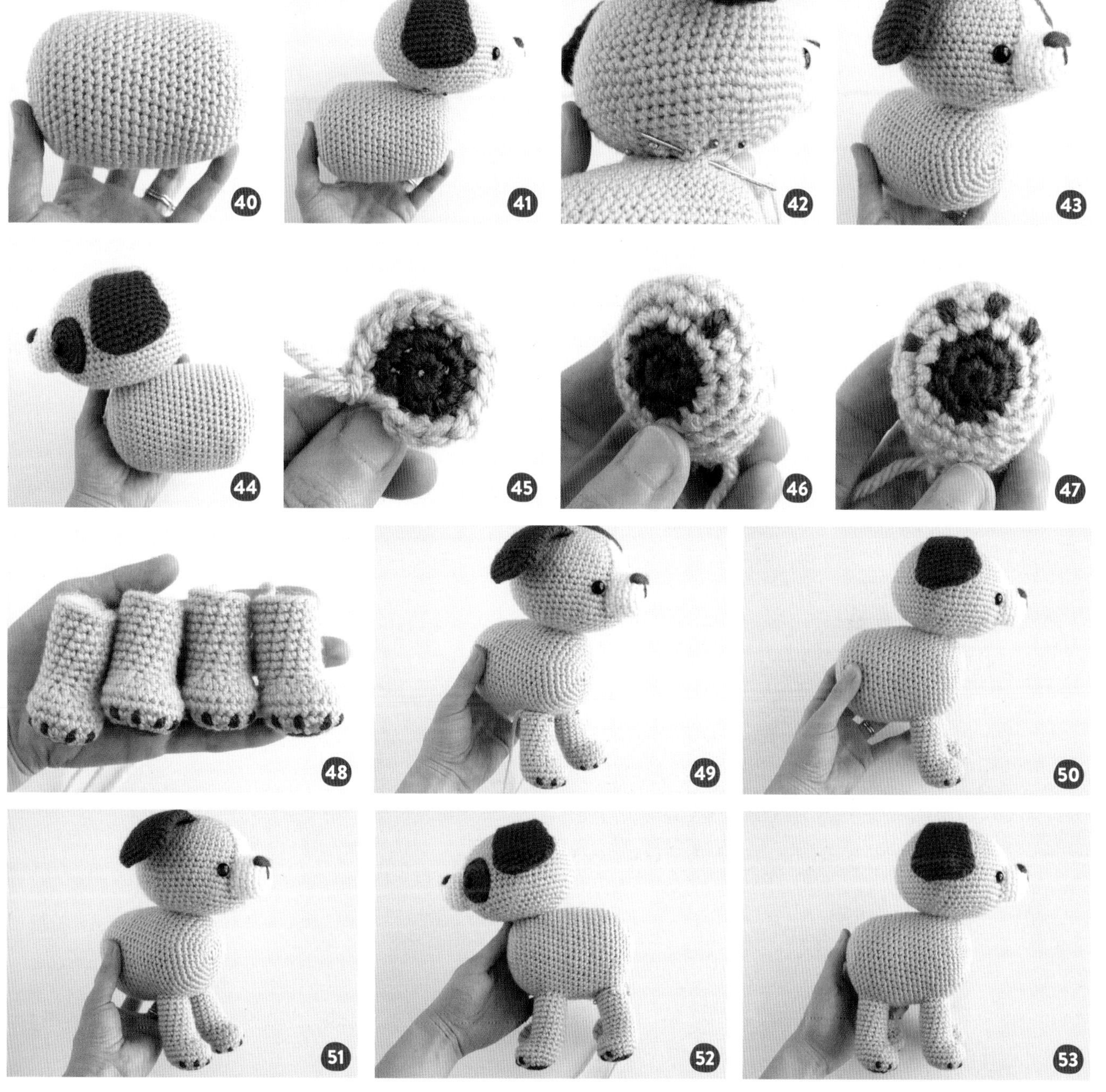
40
41
42
43
44
45
46
47
48
49
50
51
52
53

TAIL

Using dark brown yarn,

R1	6 sc in magic ring. (6 sts)
R2	*Sc 1, inc* 3 times. (9 sts)
R3+4	Sc 9.
R5	*Sc 2, inc* 3 times. (12 sts)

Change to tan yarn,

R6-15	Sc 12.

Fasten off and leave a tail for sewing. Add fiberfill to the tail. (photo 54)

Using straight pins, pin the tail to the body between rounds 28-31. (photo 55) With the yarn needle and the tail, sew the tail into place on the body. Secure with a knot and hide inside the body. (photo 56)

COLLAR

Using red yarn,

R1	Ch 40 then starting in the 2nd ch from the hook, hdc in each chain across. (39 sts) (photos 57+58)

Fasten off and leave a tail for sewing.

Note: If the collar is too small or too big to fit around your dog's neck, simply make less or more chains at the start of row 1 as needed.

DOG TAG

Using gold yarn,

R1	8 sc in magic ring. (8 sts)

Fasten off and leave a tail for sewing. Weave in the starting tail. (photo 59)

There are two different ways to attach the collar. One is to use the leftover tails to sew it together and the second is to use hot glue. I prefer to use hot glue for this but do whatever method you prefer. Just make sure to secure all the tails at the end.

If sewing, with the yarn needle and the tail, sew the gold tag to the middle of the collar. Wrap the collar around the neck. Then, using the tail from the collar, sew the two ends of the collar together. Secure and weave in the tails.

If using hot glue, start by weaving in all the tails. Wrap the collar around the neck and apply a tiny bit of glue to one end. (photo 60) Then press the other end to connect the collar. Apply a tiny dot of glue to the back of the gold tag and place on top of where the two edges of the collar meet. This will hide the seam. (photos 61-63)

54

55

56

GUINEA PIG

INTERMEDIATE

FINISHED MEASUREMENTS

- Approx. 4 inches wide by 4 inches tall by 7 inches long

MATERIALS

- Worsted weight yarn: Honey and White
- Size F/3.75mm crochet hook
- One pair of 10mm safety eyes
- Brown embroidery floss and needle
- Polyester fiberfill stuffing
- Yarn needle
- Scissors
- Stitch marker
- Straight pins

ABBREVIATIONS

- Ch- Chain
- Inc- Increase
- Inv Dec- Invisible Decrease
- R- Round/Row
- Sc- Single Crochet
- St/s- Stitch/es

Note: The guinea pig body has a lot of color changes. I found it best to cut the yarn after each color change and rejoin it when needed. Just make sure to secure all the ends if you do this method. Another option is to carry the yarn behind the work and pick it up when needed. I didn't like this method, as the yarn being carried was visible through the stitches. Remember to leave loose tension on the color not being used if you do this method.

BODY

Using white yarn,

R1 6 sc in magic ring. (6 sts)
R2 Inc in each st around. (12 sts)
R3 *Sc 2, inc* 4 times. (16 sts)

Change to honey,

R4 Sc 3, inc, sc 2, with white sc 1, inc, sc 3, with honey inc, sc 3, inc. (20 sts)
R5 With honey sc 8, with white sc 1, inc, sc 3, with honey sc 6, inc. (22 sts)
R6 With honey sc 9, with white sc 1, inc, sc 2, with honey sc 8, inc. (24 sts)
R7 With honey *sc 3, inc* 2 times, sc 2, with white sc 1, inc, sc 2, with honey sc 1, inc, *sc 3, inc* 2 times. (30 sts)
R8 With honey *sc 4, inc* 2 times, sc 4, with white inc, sc 1, with honey sc 3, inc, *sc 4, inc* 2 times. (36 sts)
R9 With honey sc 17, with white sc 2, with honey sc 17. (36 sts)
R10 With honey sc 8, inc, sc 8, with white inc, sc 1, with honey sc 7, inc, sc 8, inc. (40 sts)
R11 With honey sc 9, inc, sc 9, with white inc, with honey *Sc 9, inc* 2 times. (44 sts)
R12 With honey sc 21, with white sc 1, with honey sc 22. (44 sts) Fasten off the white yarn and secure with a knot.

Continuing with honey yarn,

R13 *Sc 10, inc* 4 times. (48 sts)
R14+15 Sc 48.

Add the safety eyes between rounds 8 and 9, placing them about 16 stitches apart. (photo 1)

With brown embroidery floss, make the nose/mouth. Insert the needle from the inside, near round 3, and pull through to the outside. Leaving about 1 stitch in between, insert the needle into the head. Pull the needle through, but not all the way. You'll want to leave a small "U" shape. (photos 2+3) Go down past the magic ring and pull the needle through to the outside. (photo 4) Leave about 1 stitch in between and insert the needle into the head again. (photo 5) Pull the needle through, leaving another "U" shape, this one will be upside down. (photo 6) Next, take the needle and pull through to the outside right near the top of the magic ring, coming over the first "U". (photo 7) Then go down to the other side of the magic ring and insert the needle into the head. Make sure to go around the second "U". (photo 8) Pull the needle through the head to bring the "U's" into a "V" shape.

If there is slack on any part, just pull the thread taut on each part (the first U, second U, and the vertical line) until all parts lie flat against the nose area. (photo 9) Secure the floss with a knot and hide inside the head.

R16 *Sc 10, inv dec* 4 times. (44 sts)
R17 Sc 44.
R18 *Sc 9, inv dec* 4 times. (40 sts)
R19 *Sc 8, inv dec* 4 times. (36 sts)
R20 *Sc 8, inc* 4 times. (40 sts)

R21 *Sc 9, inc* 4 times. (44 sts)
R22 *Sc 10, inc* 4 times. (48 sts)
R23 *Sc 11, inc* 4 times. (52 sts)
R24+25 Sc 52.

Add fiberfill to the head only, waiting to add the rest until after round 37.

Use photos 10-13 as a reference as you work the color changes.

R26 With honey sc 10, with white sc 19, with honey sc 23. (52 sts)
R27 With honey sc 10, with white sc 20, with honey sc 22. (52 sts)
R28 With honey sc 11, with white sc 20, with honey sc 21. (52 sts)
R29+30 With honey sc 10, with white sc 21, with honey sc 21. (52 sts)

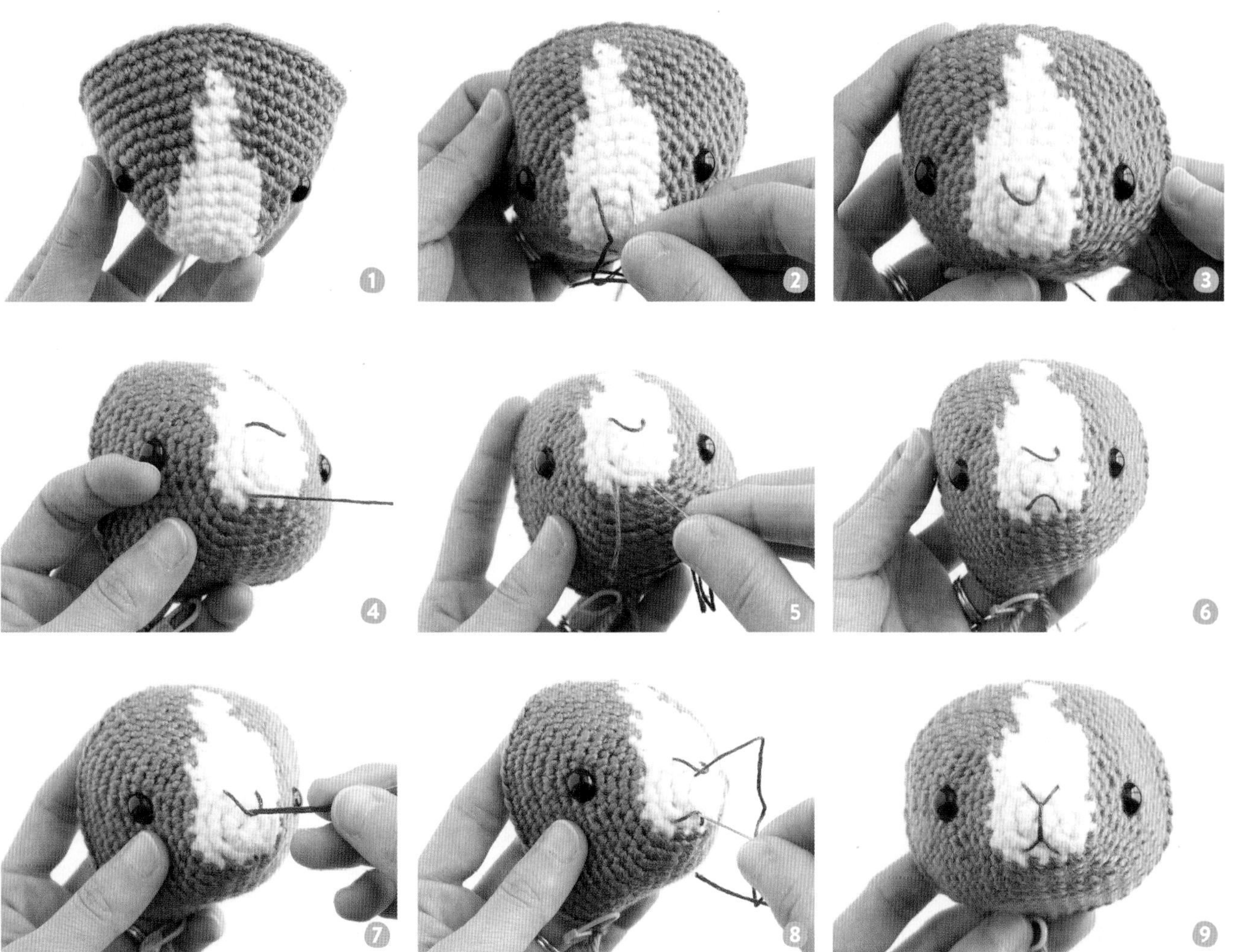

R31	With honey sc 10, with white sc 22, with honey sc 20. (52 sts)
R32	With honey sc 11, with white sc 22, with honey sc 19. (52 sts)
R33	With honey sc 11, with white sc 21, with honey sc 20. (52 sts)
R34	With honey sc 12, with white sc 20, with honey sc 20. (52 sts)
R35	With honey sc 11, inv dec, with white sc 11, inv dec, sc 5, with honey sc 6, inv dec, sc 11, inv dec. (48 sts)
R36	With honey sc 12, with white sc 16, with honey sc 20. (48 sts) Fasten off the white yarn and secure with a knot.

Continuing with honey yarn,

R37	*Sc 6, inv dec* 6 times. (42 sts)

Begin adding fiberfill to the body and continue adding as you close the piece.

R38	Sc 42.
R39	*Sc 5, inv dec* 6 times. (36 sts)
R40	Sc 36.
R41	*Sc 4, inv dec* 6 times. (30 sts)
R42	Sc 30.
R43	*Sc 3, inv dec* 6 times. (24 sts)
R44	*Sc 2, inv dec* 6 times. (18 sts)
R45	*Sc 1, inv dec* 6 times. (12 sts)
R46	Inv dec around 6 times. (6 sts)

Fasten off and leave a tail to close the piece. (photos 14-17)

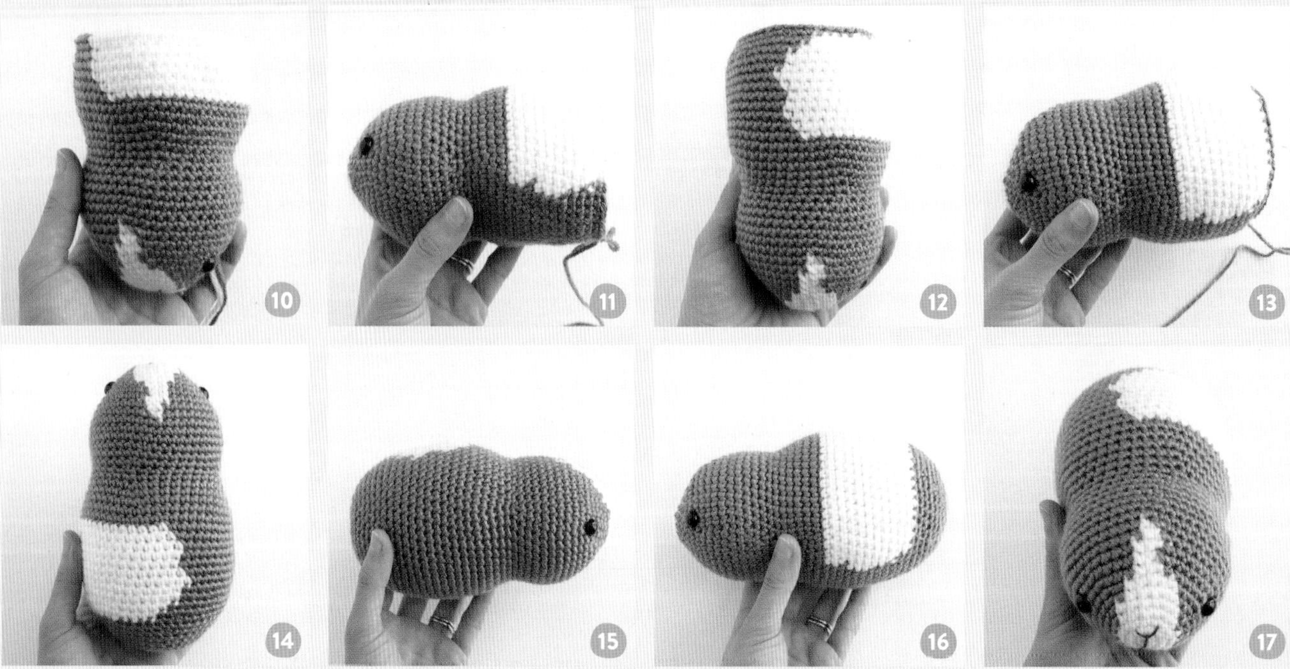

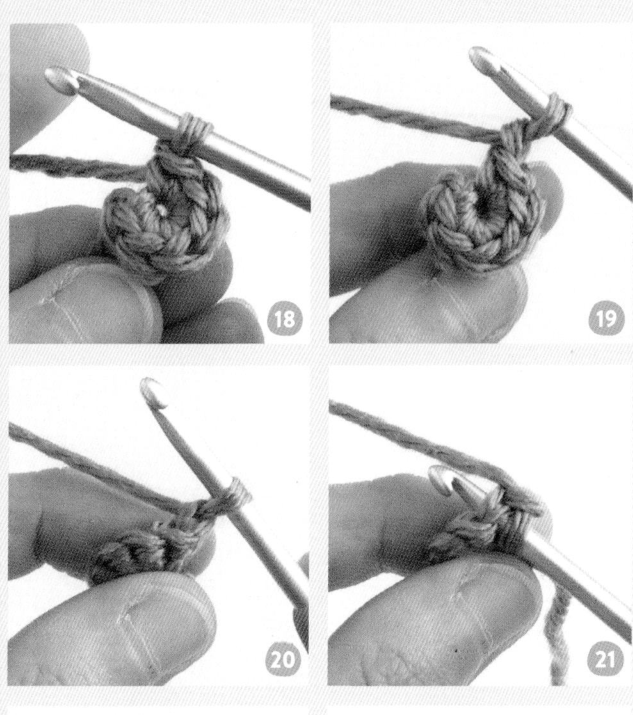

EARS: MAKE 2

Using honey yarn,

R1 6 sc in magic ring. (6 sts) Ch 1 and turn. (photos 18-20)

R2 Inc in the next two sts, 3 sc into one st, 3 sc into one st, inc in the next two sts. (14 sts) (photos 21-23)

Fasten off and leave a tail for sewing. (photo 24)

Using straight pins, pin the ears to the body between rounds 14 and 15, about 8 stitches apart. (photos 25-27) With the yarn needle and the tail, sew the ears to the head. (photos 28-30) Secure with a knot and hide inside the body. Weave in the starting tail and secure as well. Where the two sets of 3 sc are, fold this part of the ear over. (photos 31-34)

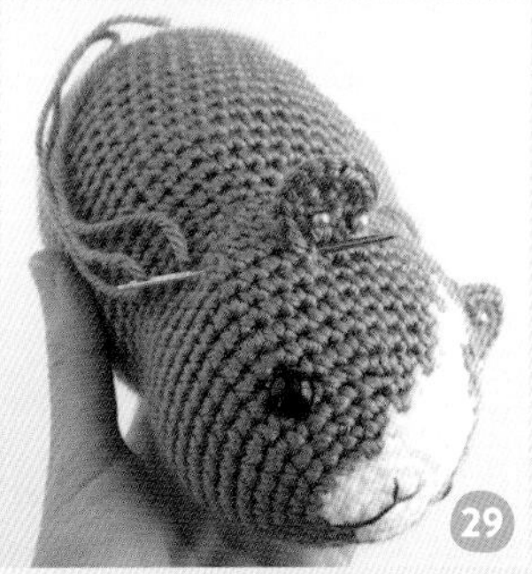

18 19 20 21 22 23 24 25 26 27 28 29

FRONT LEGS: MAKE 2

Using honey yarn,

R1	6 sc in magic ring. (6 sts)
R2	*Sc 1, inc* 3 times. (9 sts)
R3-6	Sc 9.

Fasten off and leave a tail for sewing. Add a little bit of fiberfill to the legs. (photo 35)

Using straight pins, pin the legs between rounds 23-26, about 5 to 6 stitches apart. With the yarn needle and the tail, sew the legs to the body. Secure with a knot and hide inside the body. (photos 36-38)

BACK LEGS: MAKE 2

Using honey yarn,

R1 6 sc in magic ring. (6 sts)
R2 Inc in each st around. (12 sts)
R3-8 Sc 12.

Add fiberfill to the legs, making sure to stuff lightly near round 8.

R9 *Sc 1, inv dec* 4 times. (8 sts)
R10 Sc 4. Do this by lining up the stitches on both sides of the leg, then inserting the hook into both stitches. Then sc as normal. (photos 39-42)

Fasten off and leave a tail for sewing. (photo 43)

Using straight pins, pin the legs to the body near round 39, about 3 to 4 stitches apart. (photos 44+45) With the yarn needle and the tail, sew the legs to the body. Weave the needle under both loops (the "V") from R10 of the legs and then into the body. (photo 46) Continue sewing across all of round 10.

With the same yarn tail, sew the top of the legs to the body. (photos 47-49) This helps keep the legs next to the body. Weave the needle through the top part of the leg and then into the body. Pull the needle through one of the stitch holes on the body. Then insert into the same stitch hole and weave through to the leg. Repeat until you've sewn across the entire top of the leg. (photo 50) Secure with a knot and hide inside the body. (photos 51-54)

SOLID-COLORED GUINEA PIG

For a solid-colored guinea pig, follow the pattern below for the body. The ears, nose/mouth, and both sets of legs will be the same as the multi-colored guinea pig. Reference those assembly photos when needed.

Using tan yarn,

R1 6 sc in magic ring. (6 sts)
R2 Inc in each st around. (12 sts)
R3 *Sc 2, inc* 4 times. (16 sts)
R4 *Sc 3, inc* 4 times. (20 sts)
R5 *Sc 9, inc* 2 times. (22 sts)
R6 *Sc 10, inc* 2 times. (24 sts)
R7 *Sc 3, inc* 6 times. (30 sts)
R8 *Sc 4, inc* 6 times. (36 sts)
R9 Sc 36.
R10 *Sc 8, inc* 4 times. (40 sts)
R11 *Sc 9, inc* 4 times. (44 sts)
R12 Sc 44.

Add the safety eyes between rounds 8 and 9, placing them about 16 stitches apart. With brown embroidery floss, make the nose/mouth following the directions from the multi-colored guinea pig.

R13 *Sc 10, inc* 4 times. (48 sts)
R14+15 Sc 48.
R16 *Sc 10, inv dec* 4 times. (44 sts)
R17 Sc 44.
R18 *Sc 9, inv dec* 4 times. (40 sts)
R19 *Sc 8, inv dec* 4 times. (36 sts)
R20 *Sc 8, inc* 4 times. (40 sts)
R21 *Sc 9, inc* 4 times. (44 sts)
R22 *Sc 10, inc* 4 times. (48 sts)
R23 *Sc 11, inc* 4 times. (52 sts)

Add fiberfill to the head only, waiting to add the rest until after round 37.

R24-34 Sc 52.
R35 *Sc 11, inv dec* 4 times. (48 sts)
R36 Sc 48.
R37 *Sc 6, inv dec* 6 times. (42 sts)

Begin adding fiberfill to the body and continue adding as you close the piece.

R38 Sc 42.
R39 *Sc 5, inv dec* 6 times. (36 sts)
R40 Sc 36.
R41 *Sc 4, inv dec* 6 times. (30 sts)
R42 Sc 30.
R43 *Sc 3, inv dec* 6 times. (24 sts)
R44 *Sc 2, inv dec* 6 times. (18 sts)
R45 *Sc 1, inv dec* 6 times. (12 sts)
R46 Inv dec around 6 times. (6 sts)

Fasten off and leave a tail to close the piece. (photos 55-57)

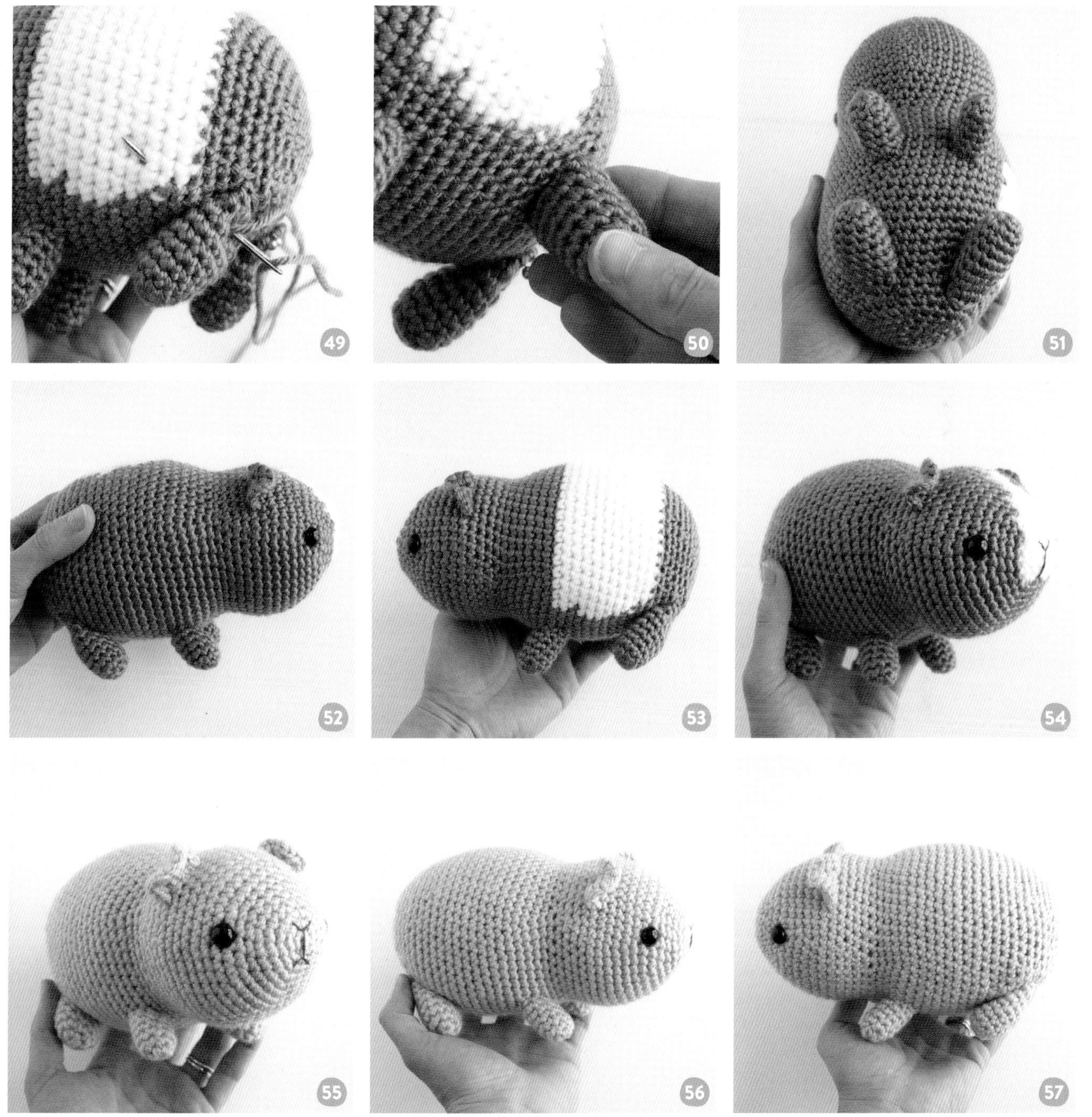
49
50
51
52
53
54
55
56
57

ACKNOWLEDGMENTS

I'm beyond grateful for all the people who helped make this book possible. Without their support, this book would still be just an idea on paper.

A massive thank you to Lindsay, Clare, Peter, Brenna, and the entire team at Blue Star Press and Paige Tate & Co. It's always an honor to work with all of you on these books. I'm so appreciative for the opportunity to share my work within these pages that you helped create. Thank you for constantly believing in me, for being flexible when I needed more time and for cheering me on during every step of writing this book.

To my incredible tech editor Carmen Nuland. I can't thank you enough for investing so much of your time in making sure these patterns were accurate and as perfect as can be. Your attention to detail and thoughtful insight has helped me create another book I am so proud of.

I had the great pleasure of working with an amazing group of pattern testers for these patterns. Abby Dalager, Andrea Thiessen, Anika Kam, Anna Hall, Anna Turek, Bianca Flatman, Christina Marie, Deidra Montalvo, Elizabeth Joersz, Jason Knop, Jenessa Davis, Lysa Rohrer, Megan Bopp, Melissa Pegan, Stephanie Cothran, Tina Shunk. Thank you for sharing not only your time and feedback with me but also your talent. Seeing each of you create these animals during testing truly made for an unforgettable experience.

I wouldn't be where I am today without my loyal and supportive followers. When I announced I was writing my fourth book, your enthusiasm pushed me to design my best work yet. Every like, share, message and purchase does not go unseen and I couldn't be more grateful for all of your support. It brings me so much joy and honor to know that some of you are picking up this book and learning to crochet from it. You are what keeps me pursuing this dream of being a crochet designer and author.

I could never express how much I appreciate my family and all their encouragement they've given me over the years. To Rachael, Taylor, Jessica, Jacob, Grandpa, and my in-laws Amy and George. Thank you for being on the sidelines cheering me on as I wrote this book. Getting to share these designs with you before anyone else saw them will always be my favorite memory.

To my mom and grandma, who are with me in spirit. Mom, I remember talking about this book with you when it was just an idea. I know you would have been so excited to see each animal as I finished them. I miss you every day and will be forever grateful for all the sacrifices you made and the support you always gave me. Grandma, you have played the most important role in my entire crochet career. If it wasn't for your generous heart, I wouldn't have fallen in love with crochet. You would have been tickled pink to see my books on the shelves of our favorite craft stores. I owe so much of my success to you.

Last but certainly not least, I want to thank my husband, Carl. You have blessed me in more ways than you will ever know. From day one you have been there to support me. You have always encouraged me to chase my dreams and are there with me every step of the way. Even on the days where all I want to do is give up. Thank you for listening to my crazy ideas (and for giving me your crazy ideas!), for being so patient with me and for being an extra pair of hands when I needed help. I'm so incredibly lucky to have you and our pups, Thunder and Storm, by my side. Love you forever, Carl!

Published by Blue Star Press
PO Box 8835, Bend, OR 97708
contact@bluestarpress.com
www.bluestarpress.com

Photography and writing by Lauren Espy
Website: www.amenagerieofstitches.com
Instagram: @amenagerieofstitches
Layout Design by Rhoda Wong

ISBN: 9781950968954

Printed in Colombia

10 9 8 7 6 5 4 3 2 1